SO-DQW-553

" *'I remember my grandparents were pioneers, but it was my grandfather who received the credit. I know that if it hadn't been for my grandmother's support, he wouldn't have done half of what he accomplished. I don't want to take away from his achievements, but I now realize how much women have contributed to the development of this country.'* "
**Kay Sanderson, Calgary Mirror, June 29, 1982**

**"The women selected represent a variety of ethnic, religious, and economic backgrounds and come from all areas of the province. 'I wanted to show the different kinds of contribution women make,' says Mrs. Sanderson, who has long felt women are neglected in history books."**
*The Calgary Herald, April 11, 1977*

*"It is said that behind every great man, there is a great woman, and after viewing the current exhibit at the Station in Okotoks, perhaps this saying can be rephrased: Behind every great province are great women. "*
**The Eagleview Point, October 18, 1988**

**"Sanderson discovered that few people have a well-defined goal in life, one that they work toward single-mindedly. Most of her women were simply 'trying to improve conditions, wherever they happened to be.' "**
*Western People, March 24, 1983*

# Canadian Cataloguing in Publication Data

Sanderson, Kay
  200 remarkable Alberta women

Biographies and portraits of 200 Alberta women, 1880-1980, to
  accompany the photo exhibit.
ISBN 0-9685832-0-2


1. Women--Alberta--Biography. 2. Women--Alberta--
Pictorial works--Exhibitions. I. Hauschildt, Elda. II. Famous 5
Foundation. III. Title. IV. Title: Two hundred remarkable
Alberta women.

HQ1459.A4S25 1999   920.72'097123   C99-901101-4

Printed and Bound in Canada

# The
# Kay Sanderson Collection

# *200*
# *Remarkable*
# *Alberta*
# *Women*

# Acknowledgements

Kay Sanderson's Collection of 200 Remarkable Alberta Women has been published through the generosity of the Thomas J. Ranaghan Foundation, which provided funds to Calgary's Famous 5 Foundation for the book's production. A further grant was provided by Margaret Randall McCready, because of her personal belief in the importance of Sanderson's work, to mount and display the photographic component of the project.

Mrs. Sanderson's archives and the accompanying photographs are housed at the Western Heritage Centre, in Cochrane, Alberta, where they will always be accessible to researchers. In the early 1980s, a collection of the photos and stories of 50 of the women included in this Collection toured Alberta, with the assistance of the Alberta Historical Resources Foundation.


**Editor:** Elda Hauschildt
**Project Committee:** Margaret Randall McCready, Nancy Millar, Elda Hauschildt, Brian McCready.
**Editorial Committee:** Elda Hauschildt, Margaret Randall McCready, Nancy Millar, Linda McClelland, Beth McKenty, Elaine Park, Wendy Clewes.
**Production Committee:** Brian McCready, Elda Hauschildt, Wendy Clewes, Margaret Randall McCready, Twyla Loney.

## Table of Contents

**Chapter 1: 1800-1875** ............................p1
**Chapter 2: 1876-1900** ...........................p25
**Chapter 3: 1901-2000** ...........................p68

# Introduction

Women's stories are "written in sand," a female historian once mused, reflecting on the fact that the history of women – who they are, where and how they lived, what they did, what they contributed to their communities and to their country – is often lost through neglect or oversight by the people who write history.

Most of us think of history as centered on important dates, on huge and dramatic events that change the course of human life. Too few consider history as a recording of the stories that make up the fabric of life, the story of where we came from, an indication of where we might be going.

Calgary's Kay Sanderson first decided to do something to stem the loss of women's histories back in 1973, when she read an article in *Chatelaine* magazine that zoned in on the idea that women's stories were not being properly told in North America. A relative newcomer to Alberta – she was born in Manitoba and lived all over the world as an air force wife – Kay decided to begin to record stories about the women who contributed to the development of her new province.

Kay applied for a Canada Council grant, and was surprised when she was allotted $1,000 for the project. That small indication of support was all she needed to set off on more than a decade of research and reporting. She looked at the project from many sides.

What women did for a living: missionary, teacher, nurse, musician, artist. What they did to help their communities develop – education, health, sports, community affairs, fundraising, the arts. What positions they obtained – school trustee, alderman, mayor, member of the legislative assembly, member of the House of Commons, member of the Senate. What community groups they organized and supported – United Farm Women, the Red Cross, Women's Institutes, churches, temperance groups, and the arts. She learned what they helped build, what they deemed important, where they lived, how they travelled, how they made friends, and how they lived and died.

By the end of a decade, Kay had collected – and archived her sources – the stories of more than 200 women who 'mattered' in the history of Alberta. She found their photographs – often with great difficulty. And sometimes, to her surprise, she found she had the only photo of a historic site. Fort Ethier, for example, was the backdrop for Margaret Morris Lucas' picture, and that turned out to be the only visual record of the fort.

Kay's archival materials and her collection of photographs are to be included in the Alberta history told at the Western Heritage Centre in Cochrane. She has achieved her aim. These women's stories will not be written in sand.

The
Kay Sanderson Collection

# *200*
# *Remarkable*
# *Alberta*
# *Women*

## CHAPTER 1: 1800-1875

# Elizabeth Chantler McDougall  1818-1903

**Elizabeth McDougall was wife, mother, homemaker, missionary, nurse, teacher, traveller, and foster mother to anyone in need of help.**

She was raised a Quaker in England, but became a Wesleyan Methodist after a religious experience at a revival meeting in Canada. Rev. George McDougall was a Scottish Presbyterian, but also became Wesleyan Methodist after a similar experience. Elizabeth married George in 1842, and they came to Alberta in 1863.

Elizabeth was a strong supporter of her husband's work among the aboriginals in Ontario, Manitoba, and Alberta. The couple had nine children and sent them all to eastern Ontario for education because Elizabeth believed in education for both boys and girls. Often alone but not easily discouraged, she carried on in spite of great hardship, isolation, and ever-present possibility of attack. Her duties included family and home, services for women at the Morley Mission, nursing the sick, and mediating disputes. Elizabeth had the ability to instill courage in others and was a source of strength to early pioneer women. After her husband's death of a heart attack while hunting buffalo, she remained at Morley carrying on his missionary work. She died there, and both are buried in the mission cemetery

# Sister Emery (Zoe Leblanc) 1826-1885

**Under Sister Emery's guidance the Grey Nuns, as they were known, established Alberta's first institutions: a boarding school, an orphanage, a hospital, and a home for the aged.**

Three Sisters of Charity, Sisters Lamy and Alphonse and their superior Sister Emery (Zoe Leblanc), arrived at Lac Ste. Anne, a Metis community northwest of Fort Edmonton, on September 24, 1859. They had followed the fur-trade route from their Montreal convent to St. Boniface, and from there they had used a Red River cart during a seven-week trip. At Lac Ste. Anne, the trio encountered food shortages and struggled with the Cree language, but they persisted. In 1863, their mission was moved to St. Albert, and the nuns grew a garden in the rich soil to supplement their scant diet

Sister Emery's special training was as a nurse, and her medical skills were put to their greatest test in the small-pox epidemic of 1869/70. Over 300 people, one-third of the settlement, died. Fortunately, the Sisters had added a hospital ward, probably the first hospital building in Alberta. By 1883 the Sisters cared for 30 children, feeding them, educating them, even weaving and sewing their clothing. Sister Emery continued to serve the mission until her death in 1885.

# Jane Gibb Stafford 1842-1925

**Jane Gibb Stafford, the mother of 14 children, witnessed the transformation of the coal-mining camp of Coalbanks into the city of Lethbridge.**

Scottish-born, Jane Gibb married William Stafford there in 1863 and had seven children before emigrating to Canada. An infant daughter died in Scotland. The Staffords had four more children in Nova Scotia before William and their eldest son, Henry, went west, where William was Coalbanks superintendent of mines. Jane and the other children arrived from Nova Scotia in June, 1883. They ended the train trip riding the caboose of a construction train, transferring to a democrat wagon for the last 100 miles from Dunsmore siding (near Medicine Hat).

The eldest son, Henry, died at Coalbanks soon after Jane arrived. There was no clergy, no undertaker, no cemetery. The miners built the coffin, William read the service, and Henry was buried in the river bottom. Three more Stafford children were born at Coalbanks, and Jane held the first church services there in her home. She always welcomed visitors and took great interest in the welfare of the pioneers and aboriginal residents of the area.

# Jane Smith Winder 1846-1926

**Jane Smith Winder spent an exciting decade, 1876 to 1885, in the Fort Macleod area, where her husband was first a member of the North West Mounted Police (NWMP) and then a rancher.**

Born and married in Quebec, the Winders spent the first years of their marriage in California, where their first son was born. They returned to Quebec in 1872, and a daughter was born there. William joined the NWMP in 1873, coming west in 1874; the family joined him at Fort Macleod in 1876, living in a cottonwood house within the fort. Jane and the other NWMP wives faced frontier life with courage, often left on their own in the fort while their husbands were away on duty. A second son was born to the Winders at Fort Macleod in 1879.

By 1881, William had retired from the NWMP and started ranching on a huge scale, leasing 500,000 acres and raising horses and cattle. Jane and the family lived in the village, although she went home to Quebec for the birth of her fourth child, a daughter, in 1884. William died in 1885, and Jane took the three youngest back to Quebec; their oldest son, George, continued to ranch. Jane died in Lennoxville, Quebec in 1926.

# Eliza McDougall Hardisty 1849-1929

**Elizabeth McDougall Hardisty was one of only six white women to sign the Treaty No. 7 at Blackfoot Crossing in 1877.**

After studying at Wesleyan Female College, Hamilton, Ontario, Eliza McDougall joined her family at Victoria on the North Saskatchewan River, where her father had established a Methodist mission two years earlier. At 16 years, she adapted well to the hardships of mission life, helping out in the school and playing the church melodeon.

She met Richard Hardisty, a Hudson's Bay Company employee, and married him on September 21, 1866. Peter Erasmus, a friend, said: "Her honeymoon trip by cart to Edmonton and saddle horse to Rocky Mountain House was an event of historical fortitude that any present-day bride might well envy."

In 1871 Richard was appointed chief factor at Fort Edmonton, and Eliza became chatelaine of the post, enjoying a rich social life as Edmonton's first lady and later signing the treaty at Blackfoot Crossing. In 1883 the family moved to Calgary for two years, then returned to Edmonton, where in 1888 Richard was appointed Alberta's first Senator.

# Henrietta Muir Edwards  1849-1931

**Henrietta Edwards was legal advisor to the Famous 5, the group of Alberta women whose long battle in the courts led to Canadian women being granted the status of 'persons.' An expert on laws relating to women and children, she compiled and published summaries of the laws:** *Legal Status of Women in Alberta* **in 1917 and** *Legal Status of Women in Canada* **in 1924.**

Henrietta came to Alberta in 1903 when her husband, Oliver Cromwell Edwards, was posted as medical officer to the Blood tribe. At 54, Henrietta had more than 30 years' experience in working to improve conditions for working girls. She and her sister had founded a Working Girls' Club in Montreal in 1875 to provide meal services, reading rooms, and study classes. They also published a periodical, *The Working Women of Canada*, which drew attention to the plight of these girls. The project, undertaken at their own expense, was funded chiefly from their earnings as artists.

Henrietta was a gifted miniature portraitist and china painter. In 1893, at the request of the Canadian government, she had painted a set of dishes for inclusion in the Canadian Exhibit at the Chicago World Fair.

# Jean Drever Pinkham  1849-1940

**The daughter of Red River pioneers, Jean Drever Pinkham continued the pioneering spirit, helping to establish Calgary's first general hospital, the Victorian Order of Nurses (VON), and the first Calgary chapter of the Imperial Order of Daughters of the Empire (IODE).**

Jean Ann Drever grew up at Red River, where she married a young Anglican clergyman, William Pinkham, in 1868. They had seven children, the eldest of whom died at six weeks. When William was named the Bishop of Calgary in 1889, the family moved further west. William travelled a great deal as bishop. Jean raised the family, had an eighth child, and worked tirelessly for community organizations. She was largely responsible for establishing the first general hospital in Calgary, and then organized the Women's Hospital Aid Society to keep the new hospital going.

Later Jean helped organize the VON and chaired the first meeting of the Local Council of Women. She was also the first regent of the first Calgary IODE chapter. The Pinkhams worshipped in Calgary's first Anglican church, a wooden building, until 1905, and then in the new sandstone Pro-Cathedral. Jean was honorary president of the Pro-Cathedral Women's Auxiliary.

# Caroline Hamilton Gaetz   (died in 1906)

**Though married only once, Nova Scotia born Caroline Hamilton Gaetz led two lives: one as a minister's wife, and the second as the wife of a farmer and merchant.**

Her husband, Leonard Gaetz, was a successful Methodist minister who held charges in some of the largest churches in Canada before illness forced him from the ministry in 1883. In 1884, he brought his wife and 10 children west. There he homesteaded and planned to open a trading post in the Red Deer area. Caroline gave birth to the 11th Gaetz child in their new home. The family was successful, and two years later Leonard purchased a portable mill and covered their log home with lumber, shingling the roof.

By 1890, the Gaetz family moved into a large home in Red Deer, where they were stalwart members of the local Methodist Church. Caroline organized the Methodist Church Ladies Aid, the first organized group of women in Red Deer, in 1892. Five years later, Leonard returned to the ministry, and he and Caroline served in Brandon and Winnipeg. On their retirement in 1901, they returned to Red Deer.

# Zina Young Card 1850-1931

**Trekking 800 miles by covered wagon from Utah, Zina Young Card arrived in southern Alberta in summer 1887 and set about helping her husband, Charles Ora Card, found the first Church of Jesus Christ of Latter Day Saints settlement in the province.**

The Cards brought 10 families with them, and the settlement was named Cardston.

Zina Card, a daughter of Brigham Young, helped guide and support the new community. Besides raising her family and carrying out religious duties, she used money from her father's estate to fund many early Cardston projects: church buildings, a two-storey high school, and a cheese factory, among others.

Aunt Zina, as she was called, was loved for her benevolent spirit and for her warm and motherly nature. Her log home, dubbed the 'Cotton Flannel Palace' by Charles because she had lined its walls with richly coloured flannel, was known for a hospitality that extended beyond the community to aboriginals, police and government officials, and neighbouring families.

# Olive Blewett Ross 1850-1932

**Olive Blewett Ross, wife to Edmonton's first hotelier, started married life in a log cabin near the shaft of her husband's coal mine.**

English-born, Olive Blewett came to Canada as a child and to Edmonton in 1878. There she met and married Donald Ross, who mined for coal below what is 101st Street in Edmonton today. Her wedding ring was made from gold washed from the gravel of the North Saskatchewan river. Donald became a hotelkeeper, and the Edmonton Hotel was reputed to be the first built west of Brandon, Manitoba. Ross' hotel became a meeting place for newcomers. During the Yukon gold rush, the hotel was so crowded people competed to sleep on the billiard tables.

Olive and Donald had three children: James, Olive (Dolly), and Donald, all born in Edmonton. Olive was a keen gardener and was well-known locally for the variety of produce that she grew. Active in community and church affairs, Olive was 82 when she died in Edmonton, her home for more than 54 years.

# Annie McKenzie McDougall  1850-1939

**Annie McDougall, Morley pioneer and business woman, was one of six white women to sign Treaty No. 7 at Blackfoot Crossing. She is also sometimes described as the first business woman between Fort Garry and the Pacific because she was in charge of trading during her husband's long trips away.**

The daughter of Scottish immigrants, Annie married David McDougall in July 1871 in Rat Creek, Manitoba. Their honeymoon was a 1,000-mile trip by buckboard to Victoria Mission in Alberta. When John McDougall started a mission among the Stoney, David decided to start a trading post there. Annie and their first baby made the trip of 13 days in a horse-drawn carriole in 45 below zero weather.

Fear of attack, the isolation, and the great scarity of everything made life very harsh for Annie. But she also witnessed the last buffalo hunt and more than once, took part in the chase. She was a good horsewoman, keen sportswoman, and known for her kindness and willingness to help others. Annie had six children: one died in infancy. She died from injuries received in a car accident driving back to Calgary from the New York World's Fair in June, 1939.

# Mary Drever Macleod  1852-1933

**Mary Drever Macleod, another of the six white women who signed Treaty No. 7, was known for her beauty and vibrant wit. She was also known for her resilience.**

She came in 1877 to live at Fort Macleod, the Northwest Mounted Police (NWMP) post that her husband, the commissioner, had established on the Oldman River. Their house, like all buildings in the hastily erected community, lacked much in the way of conveniences. It had been inadvertently built over an old buffalo trail. When it rained, a small but steady stream coursed through.

The hardships and responsibilities of establishing a frontier home held no terrors for Mary. When her husband, also magistrate for the Northwest Territories, rode off on a tour of duty, Mary often went with him. Thus, she signed the 1877 Treaty. When Mary gave birth to the first of her five children, a Mounted Police surgeon attended. Macleod resigned to become a full-time magistrate, moving the family to Pincher Creek where he began to raise horses for the NWMP. Judicial duties took too much of his time, and the venture failed. The Macleods were respected and recognized as one of the area's first families.

# Elizabeth McDougall Young  1852-1945

**In her life, Elizabeth Young, daughter of Rev. George and Elizabeth McDougall, marvelled at buffalo stampeding across the prairie and at airplane roaring over Edmonton during World War II.**

Elizabeth came to Alberta with her family in 1863, when she was almost 11. She attended school in Ontario, including the Wesleyan Female College in Hamilton, before returning to the mission in Morley in 1870. She then spent some time caring for her widowed brother John and his children before marrying Harrison Young in 1873.

For nine years the Youngs lived at Lesser Slave Lake, where Harrison was in charge of the Hudson's Bay Company post. Elizabeth spoke Cree fluently and made friends easily. They spent four years at Lac La Biche, and it was here that, alone at the post, Libby was warned by friends of the approach of Big Bear's men during the North West Rebellion. She and the children hid in the woods for a week.

The Youngs had nine children; three died before adulthood. They lived mostly in Edmonton between 1887 and 1909. Elizabeth had been the last chatelaine of Fort Edmonton.

# Alexandra Sissons Hargreave  1853-1932

**Travelling hundreds of miles by canoe or dogsled, talking with the Cree in their language, and living in remote and difficult circumstances were all ordinary occurrences for Alexandra Sissons Hargreave.**

When she arrived in Medicine Hat in 1883 with her five small children, 31-year-old Lexie was already a seasoned pioneer, having lived at Cumberland House and Fort Frances with her husband, James, a Hudson's Bay Company (HBC) clerk. James resigned from the Company in 1882 and became a trader and rancher in the Medicine Hat area. Lexie adapted quickly to her new life, raising eight children and taking on numerous duties as a ranching wife. She often had Metis or aboriginal women to help her and saw to it that all her children learned Cree.

Lexie's 1875 marriage to James had not been a propitious one. James was seriously ill and had small hope of survival; the marriage took place at his bedside. Lexie, however, was a determined nurse who soon brought about his recovery. Fifty years later, their golden wedding anniversary was attended by 200 friends, old HBC acquaintances, business associates, ranching neighbours, government officials, relatives, and native and Metis friends.

# Elizabeth Boyd McDougall  1854-1941

**Elizabeth was the wife and helpmate of pioneering missionary John McDougall. She witnessed the signing of Treaty No. 7 at Blackfoot Crossing, and during her widowhood in Calgary was instrumental in starting the Young Women's Christian Association.**

Elizabeth's mother was sister to Rev. George McDougall and John McDougall, her cousin, was a widower with three small girls. They married in 1872; travelling from the Red River to Victoria Mission they encountered prairie fire, threatening Sioux, icy rivers, and a fierce blizzard. Determined to share in all of her husband's work, she accompanied him in the fall of 1873 when he set out to establish Morley Mission among the Stoney. The first years were very difficult, there was an acute shortage of almost everything, always the possibility of trouble with unfriendly natives, and isolation. They lived at the Morley Mission for 25 years and her seven children were all born there.

The McDougalls retired to Calgary in 1899 and were largely responsible for the building of the first Protestant church there. Their home was called *Nekenon* (our home), and Lizzie held a reception there each year on her birthday.

# Elizabeth Barrett  (died in 1888)

**Teaching in Orono, Ontario in 1874, Elizabeth Barrett heard there was a need for ministers, teachers, and helpers for the missions in Western Canada. She volunteered and spent the rest of her working life in the west.**

Her first assignment was at Whitefish Lake Mission, 100 mile northeast of Fort Edmonton, where she learned to speak Cree. She wrote home that kindness will win their favour and esteem but learning their language was the way to reach the Crees' hearts. From Whitefish, she went to Morley Mission. She was one of the six white women who signed the 1877 Treaty No. 7 at Blackfoot Crossing. At Morley, Elizabeth began learning the Stoney language and studied Stoney customs and culture.

When she was assigned to Fort Macleod, she opened a public school there, southern Alberta's first. She also held the first Methodist services at Fort Macleod. Following furloughs to the east because of illness and deaths in her family, Elizabeth returned to Morley Mission. In 1888, she became ill and died there a short time later. Elizabeth Barrett Elementary School in Cochrane is named for this pioneer teacher, who is thought to be Alberta's first professionally trained female school teacher.

# Caroline Esther Edgelaw Strong  (died in 1897)

**Caroline Esther Strong, a cultured English woman, was left a widow with eight children to raise only four years after arriving in Saskatchewan's Qu'Appelle Valley.**

Mrs. Strong (no record verifies her first name) emigrated from London in 1885 with her husband, Robert Strong, a lawyer, and her first six children. Robert died suddenly four years later, and she was left with little money and two additional children to raise. Her solution was to take the six youngest children to an isolated homestead, two and a half miles north of Walsh.

There they eked out a living, building a rough house and housing their few cows and horses in a dug-out barn. Determined to educate her children, Mrs. Strong used the Bible, Shakespeare's plays, and the writings of Charles Kingsley, Sir Walter Scott, Charles Dickens, Roman and Greek mythology, and fairy tales to teach them. When fire destroyed the house in 1895, she moved the three youngest children in with her son Charles, who as Walsh station master, lived in two boxcars. The other two boys dug a hole into a farm hillside and continued farming. The hardships and poverty of pioneering took their toll, and she died in her early 40s in 1897.

# Jemima McKay Bray  (died in 1925)

**Jemima McKay Bray recorded a number of firsts in the North West Mounted Police (NWMP): hers was one of the first police weddings in the North West Territories, she became one of the first police wives to live in Alberta, and she gave birth to the first child believed to be born into the force.**

When the NWMP arrived at what was to be Fort Walsh in 1875, they were surprised to find Edward McKay and his family, including Jemina, one of five daughters, living nearby. Edward, a former buffalo-hunter and Red River settler, had re-located to the area without formal homesteading permission. Jemima married John Bray at Fort Walsh in 1876, but they were soon transferred to Fort Macleod, where she became one of the first police wives in the province. The birth of Flora Bray at Fort Macleod, as 'close as records can prove' was another first for the force.

The Brays lived at Pincher Creek from 1881 to 1892, with Sergeant Bray taking his discharge in 1883. The family's final move was to Medicine Hat in 1892. Jemima gave birth to 12 more children after Flora.

# Jane Flett McKay 1857-1947

**Jane Flett, the daughter of an Orkney Islander father and a Cree mother, spent a decade as interpreter and nurse for her medical doctor husband, William Morrison McKay, in Hudson's Bay Company posts in the Mackenzie River and Peace River areas.**

Born December, 1857 at La Pierre's House, a company post north of the Arctic Circle, Jane grew up trained in both her parents' cultures. She married in 1874, and her husband became Alberta's first resident doctor. Conditions were primitive and medical supplies almost non-existent as the McKays tended their patients. Often, they had only three drugs for medications: rhubarb, Epsom salts, and grey powder (mercury and chalk).

But medical assistant was not Jane's only role: she was mother to 13 children, 12 of whom survived. A skilled seamstress, she made the family's clothing, using Hudson's Bay yard goods as well as hides and animal skins. Legend has it that she once sewed up a gash in a patient's abdomen because her sewing skills were better than her husband's. The McKays retired to Edmonton in 1898; Jane lived there for another five decades. A newspaper said on her 82nd birthday that she was a keen bridge player and an avid reader.

# Elizabeth Fisher McKillop 1858-1938

**Wife of the first clergyman to arrive in Lethbridge, Elizabeth Fisher McKillop was known as a woman of great energy, keen humour, deep faith, and devotion to the needs of others.**

Born in Renfrew County, Ontario, she met Presbyterian minister Charles McKillop and married him in 1881. Five years later, Charles decided to go west as a missionary, and Elizabeth and their two children followed in 1887. Elizabeth brought with her Lethbridge's first piano and first washing machine.

As the first clergyman in the city, Charles preached to a congregation of Anglicans, Catholics, Baptists, and Methodists, and Elizabeth took on the duties of minister's wife with courage and determination. Active in community affairs, especially music, Elizabeth was involved in activities at both Knox and Southminister United churches. She was known for her capacity for friendship and her ability to instill courage in others. In later years, she was often asked to speak about pioneer life in the West.

The mother of eight, Elizabeth lost two sons in infancy and a daughter to appendicitis at age 17. In 1954, the new United church was named McKillop United, in honour of both Charles and Elizabeth.

# Mary Ellen Bower Birtles, O.B.E. 1858-1943

**Ellen Birtles, a pioneer nurse in both Alberta and Manitoba, devoted her life to nursing patients and nursing students.**

Born in England, she came to Canada with her family in 1883, settling near Brandon. By 1886, she had decided to enter nursing and went to Winnipeg expecting a nursing school at the hospital there. There was none, so she started training on the job. A year later, Winnipeg opened the first nursing school in Western Canada; Ellen became one of its first three graduates. By 1890 she was on staff at the new Medicine Hat General Hospital, dividing nursing and domestic tasks with her Matron, Grace Louise Reynolds. Ellen tended the furnace as well as patients.

In 1892, she moved to the new hospital in Brandon, and then went to Calgary in 1894, as Lady Superintendent at Calgary General. There she started the province's second school of nursing, displaying her talents for organization and management. Under her guidance, and despite shortages of money, staff, and equipment, the hospital and school flourished.

Ellen kept detailed diaries which are vital historical documents on western pioneer nursing. In 1935, she received an Order of the British Empire.

# Lovisa Amey McDougall   (died in 1943)

**Travelling about the prairies in 1878 with her new husband, Ontario-born Lovisa Amey McDougall learned first-hand about trading, aboriginal culture, prairie fires and storms, and roughing it by sleeping on the ground or in other traders' shacks.**

A depressed fur trade that year drove John Alexander McDougall into debt and made him doubt that Lovisa would go through with their March marriage. She did, and they headed west to trade. They were successful enough to afford the luxury of buying a covered wagon for the return trip to Winnipeg in the fall. When John decided they should move permanently to Edmonton the next year, Lovisa helped him trade his way back across the prairies again. In Edmonton they turned a two-storey building into both their home and a trading post. By 1890, the couple had five children, and Lovisa was singing in the church choir and taking turns as organist.

John McDougall became a successful, wealthy man, and built an Edmonton mansion for Lovisa, who had helped him pay off his debts from the fur trade and re-establish his career. Their home became a social centre in the growing city.

# Lady Isabella Hardisty Lougheed 1859-1936

Belle Hardisty Lougheed was well suited to being a frontier hostess. Growing up in outposts but educated at Wellesley College in Hamilton meant she had the formal social skills of most young ladies, mixed with a refreshing adaptability and informality.

When she married James Lougheed in 1884, Calgary was a bustling town of wooden establishments and high hopes. James, a lawyer, saw a great future for Calgary and was to take an active part in its growth. He and Belle, daughter of Chief Factor William Hardisty, set up house in an abandoned tailor's shop on Stephen Ave. Outfitted with furniture from Montreal, the little house became the centre of social activity.

In 1889 James became a Senator, and in 1901 the family moved to Beaulieu, a large sandstone house on the outskirts of the city. In 1916, James was knighted, and Lady Belle was hostess to many government officials and royal family members. Her chief concerns were her growing family and her town. She was active in the Children's Aid Society, the Victorian Order of Nurses, the Imperial Order Daughters of the Empire, and was first president of the Southern Alberta Pioneers and Old Timers' Association.

# Anne Richards White  (born 1859)

**Anne Richards White was a true pioneer, helping to bring in her homestead's first crop in 1886, and then spending the winter alone after fire destroyed the harvest and forced her husband to work in the city.**

Welsh-born, Anne Richards came to Winnipeg in 1882; two years later she married Scotsman Christopher White. In 1885, she and her baby joined her father on his homestead near Red Deer, making the final leg of the trip from Calgary in a Red River cart. Since there were no accommodations for a woman and a child, they spent their first night in the police barracks at Fort Normandeau.

A year later, Christopher established his own homestead in the Clearview district, and together the couple harvested a first crop. Christopher scythed and Anne gathered and stooked. A prairie fire destroyed the results of their work, and Christopher had to go to Calgary to work as a carpenter. Anne stayed on the homestead that winter, exchanging lessons in pioneering for lessons in crocheting with a Metis neighbour, Mrs. Cook.

With patience and persistence, the Whites built up a successful operation, Murdisson Ranch, and raised a family of four. Anne was a charter member of the Clearview Women's Institute, organized in 1913.

# Margaret Morrison Lucas 1860-1922

**Margaret Lucas and her husband were among the first Alberta settlers to take advantage of the newly constructed Trans-Canada Railroad.**

They arrived in Calgary in July, 1884, loading their possessions, including a sewing machine, stove, bed, dresser, table and chairs ñ onto a wagon for the last leg of their journey. Their destination was Peace Hills Agency Farm, a few miles north of present-day Wetaskiwin. Frank Lucas was to be a government farm instructor. The farm was one of five stopping places for the stagecoach between the Hudson's Bay Company fort at Edmonton and the town of Calgary. The round trip took one week.

Margaret's new life was a busy one, feeding and housing those who passed through: stagecoach drivers, mail carriers, policemen, missionaries, and settlers. She baked bread in such quantities that an outside oven had to be constructed. As well as bearing and raising nine children, Margaret found time for a flower garden, and her home was the centre for many community activities, including church and school.

# Mary Newton (born 1860)

**Edmonton's first lay nurse arrived from England in the summer of 1886, to live with her clergyman brother and to regain her own health. She was soon back to work.**

Mary Newton represented an influential English nursing movement that pre-dated even Florence Nightingale and that originated in Anglican Church service. The Anglican nurses lived a religious life at St. John's House in London and went out to local hospitals for medical training. St. John's House was able to provide Nightingale with six nurses when she went off to serve in the Crimean War.

When Mary arrived at the Hermitage, her brother's Anglican mission eight miles downstream of Edmonton, she had already served as a professor at Queen Charlotte's Maternity Hospital in London. A local newspaper story about her arrival said she hoped to resume nursing if her health permitted; there was soon a log hospital at the Hermitage, and Mary was hard at work. Five years later, Mary advertised that she would hire out as nurse and midwife in private homes, for the sum of 10 dollars a week. Interestingly, Mary Newton is also credited with introducing lilacs to Alberta.

13

# Alice Jukes Jamieson 1860-1949

**When Calgary became the first city in the British Empire to appoint a woman as judge to a juvenile court, it was just the beginning for Alice Jukes Jamieson.**

More distinctions would follow. In December, 1916 she was appointed to Calgary's Women's Court, thus becoming the second police magistrate in Canada (the first was Emily Murphy in Edmonton). This appointment aroused a great deal of hostility from lawyers, judges, and police of the time. They contested Alice's right to make binding decisions as a judge on the grounds that, as a woman, she was not legally a person. The contest eventually went to the Supreme Court of Alberta, which upheld her right to hold office and confirmed that, in Alberta at least, women were persons.

Taking prejudice and opposition in her stride, Alice concerned herself with improving conditions for women and children. Vitally interested in social welfare, she was already prominent for such work. She was president of the Local Council of Women, a group devoted to such causes as mother's pensions, dower rights, child welfare, and women's suffrage. The council was one of the forces responsible for Alberta women gaining the right to vote in 1916.

# Grace Louise Reynolds Calder

**Grace Louise Reynolds Calder, the first Matron at the new Medicine Hat General Hospital in 1890, is credited with bringing the Florence Nightingale system of nursing to Alberta.**

Trained in Leeds, England by Nightingale graduates, Grace Louise emigrated to Winnipeg in 1884 and remained on staff at the Winnipeg General for four years. Next she spent two years in Washington, DC, before arriving in Medicine Hat as Matron. The Medicine Hat General, the first municipal hospital in the province, grew out of the makeshift hospital supplied by the railway in 1883 and incorporated in 1888. The new hospital opened in 1890; Grace Louise and her assistant Ellen Birtles, were too busy with patients to attend the formal opening in February.

Lacking proper equipment and maintenance help, the two women did everything, including boiling instruments in a large saucepan, with a steamer attached for towels and dressings. Resigning to marry Dr. J.G. Calder in 1891, Grace Louise continued to influence the hospital and its the nursing school. Dr. Calder died in 1909, and Grace Louise died a few years later. They were survived by a son.

# Mary Sharples Schaffer Warren 1861-1939

Mary Sharples Schaffer Warren went where no white woman had ever gone before; she went deep into the Canadian Rockies and found Maligne Lake. Or, to be more exact, since the natives of the area had known about Maligne Lake all along, she explored the area and in 1911 she officially mapped the lake.

A native of Pennsylvania, Mary came to the Banff and Lake Louise area with her botanist husband, Charles Schaffer, every summer from 1889 to 1903. After he died, Mary illustrated and compiled his botanical research into a book.

With a female companion, she continued to explore the Rocky Mountain area, but professional guides hesitated to take women on long expeditions. Finally, in 1906, Mary decided she'd lead her own expedition, never mind a guide. It was then that William Warren finally agreed to lead them through parts of the unexplored back country from Banff to Mount Robson. It wasn't easy but Mary proved to be as tough a mountaineer as most men. People from all over the United States came to the Banff area because of her books, lectures, and coloured slide presentations. In 1915, she married William Warren and moved permanently to Banff.

# Marion Coutts Carson 1861-1950

An elementary school was named after Marion Coutts Carson, in recognition of her dedicated work in the fields of public health, welfare, and education.

A pioneer social worker, Marion's deep sympathy for the unfortunate was felt in many areas. Usually it was through her leadership of local associations after the William Carson family came to Calgary in 1898. Six Carson children grew up there, and one son was killed in World War I.

In 1911, she formed the Tuberculosis (TB) Association and began her long crusade against tuberculosis, both to help patients and to eradicate the disease. In 1912 an eight-bed hospital, Calgary and Alberta's first TB hospital, was opened. Among other interests, Marion was a member of the Calgary Library Board, a Labour trustee on Calgary Public School Board from 1920 to 1924, a Labour Party member, and an active member of the Alberta Council of Child and Welfare for 27 years. She worked for free medical clinics for children and the distribution of milk to needy families. She received the King George V medal in 1935 for her work in the TB field and was Citizen of the Year for Calgary in the mid 1940s, the second woman to be so named.

# Sister Vincent (Rose de Lima Lefebre)  1862-1919

**Thirty years old when she entered the Providence Novitiate in Montreal, Sister Vincent (Rosa de Lima Lefebre) spent 25 years as a missionary in northern Alberta, establishing the St. Bernard Mission on Lesser Slave Lake in 1894.**

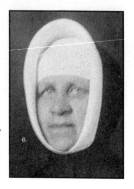

A seamstress before entering the Novitiate in 1892, Sister Vincent was on her way to northern Alberta two years later.  She led a group of five Sisters (Amedee, Theogene, Bernard, Blais, and Dugay) from Montreal; they travelled by train, wagon, and barge to reach Lesser Slave Lake, bringing with them furniture, clothing, books, and utensils.

At the mission site, they found 30 orphaned aboriginal children and set to work.  The Sisters faced isolation, harsh climate, and primitive conditions as they established the St. Bernard Mission.  Eventually, the community of Grouard grew up around the mission.  After 11 years at Grouard, Sister Vincent spent 14 years at the St. Augustine Mission at Peace River.  In January, 1919, the influenza epidemic reached the Peace River, and after nursing others for nearly three weeks, Sister Vincent died of the disease.


# Harriet Dunlop Oliver  1863-1943

**Always adventurous, Harriet Dunlop Oliver married at 18 years of age, pioneered in frontier  Edmonton, and became Ottawa hostess for Alberta's lone MP.**

Born in Ontario, Harriet arrived in Manitoba as a young child.  Her family settled near Winnipeg, and Harriet married Frank Oliver there.  It took the young couple three months by ox-cart to reach Edmonton, where Harriet set up housekeeping in a log cabin and helped her husband publish the *Edmonton Bulletin*, Alberta's first newspaper.  During the 1885 Indian uprising, most settlers sought refuge in the Hudson's Bay Company fort, but Frank decided to stay put, and Harriet and her children stayed with them.  It was a long month before troops  arrived.

The Olivers had seven children, and Harriet was a busy homemaker and community activist, helping found the first Presbyterian church in Edmonton.  She found time for adventure, taking annual trips; she and a friend rode to Banff, one year, to camp by Lake Minnewanka.  She also travelled to the Yukon and went down the Mackenzie River.  When Frank was named a federal cabinet minister in 1906, Harriet became a popular Ottawa hostess.  During the war, she travelled to England to visit one son and later visited another's French grave.

# Annie Glenn Broder (born 1937)

**Annie Broder worked steadily for over 30 years to raise musical standards in Calgary and western Canada as a music teacher, pianist, recitalist, lecturer, accompanist, and music critic.**

She was born and educated in England and was well established in European music circles before coming to Regina to marry a former Oxford professor, Richard Broder, a widower with two boys. At the invitation of Col. J. S. Dennis, she came to Calgary in 1903 "to take hold of the musical situation." She furthered choral and orchestral groups and encouraged musical education.

Annie worked untiringly to sustain interest in orchestral music between 1913/1914 and 1928, when the Calgary Symphony Orchestra was disbanded. She held annual concerts in the Palliser Hotel to give outstanding pupils an opportunity to play before the public.

She wrote a book on How to Accompany, and in 1906 composed a march titled, "*The Ride of the NWMP.*" In 1934, she represented Canada at the Anglo-American musical conference in Lausanne, Switzerland. Annie died in 1937.

# Sara Blake Lynch-Staunton 1864-1933

**Sara Blake, Alberta's first trained female painter, studied in England and lived in France before coming to Alberta to keep house for her rancher brother.**

Born in Galway, Sara studied painting at a Sussex, England convent and lived at Nice while her brother Frank went to school. She came from Europe to Pincher Creek to keep house for Frank in 1888, moving to his ranch, the Deer Horn, established in 1889. Sara began painting the Alberta landscape soon after arriving, and two of her watercolours, *Falls on the Middle Fork of the Old Man River, The Deer Horn Ranch*, are in the Glenbow art collection, Calgary.

Sara married former North West Mounted Policeman Alfred Lynch-Staunton in 1890, and moved to his homestead near Pincher Creek. The Lynch-Stauntons developed a cattle ranch and farm and raised a family of five children (three other children died young). As well as painting, Sara enjoyed reading and riding and helping with the 'tea house' during polo matches. Her husband was one of the original members of the Pincher Creek Polo Club, the first in Western Canada.

# Amanda Johnson Nilsson 1864-1940

**After Amanda Nilsson and her family emigrated from Utah to homestead at Raymond, Alberta in 1901, their house became the centre of many community activities.**

Raymond's first brass band was organized and practised there in its early years. The town's first printing press was set up in the parlour, and the *Raymond Chronicle* was printed there for some time. A vivacious and energetic lady, Amanda's wide range of interests included literary activities. She wrote articles and poems for the Chronicle and was one of the founders of Raymond's first literary club.

Although they had 13 children of their own, seven of whom survived, Amanda and Christopher were always ready to help and nurture others. Five foster children shared their home, and they sponsored a school for boys missing early education. One of their more somber contributions to the community was the provision of free coffins, built by Christopher and lined and decorated by Amanda. Coffins were much in demand in those days of high death rates. The Nilssons themselves, in one severe year, lost three children. Amanda was famous for her doughnuts sold to finance worthy causes.

# Agnes Higginson Skrine 1864-1955

**Agnes Skrine was also 'Moira O'Neill,' a famous Irish poet and writer, who wrote beautifully about life in Alberta.**

Born Agnes Higginson in County Antrim, Ireland, Agnes married Walter Skrine in 1895 and settled with him on his Bar S Ranch, 24 miles southwest of High River. Walter had 16,900 acres under lease and believed homesteaders and ranchers could be mutually helpful, an unusual idea for the time. Walter built a new, two-storey home for his bride, the lumber freighted from Calgary by teams of horses. The Skrines lived there for six years, before returning to Ireland, where Agnes, under the pseudonym 'Moira OíNeill,' wrote two books of poetry on the Glens of Antrim. Her poetry was so successful that John Mansfield, poet laureate, wrote a tribute to her when she died.

But Agnes had also written about Alberta, poetically describing the countryside. "I like the endless riding over the endless prairie, the winds sweeping the grass, the great silent sunshine, the vast skies and the splendid line of the Rockies, guarding the west," she wrote in an essay, A Lady's Life on a Ranche, in *Blackwood's Magazine*, January, 1898.

## Sister Mary Anastase 1865-1933

**A nurse, cook, and social worker, Sister Mary Anastase (Marie Vitaline Dudemaine) spent 25 years in religious service at Fort Vermillion, Peace River, Grouard, Cluny, and at the Lacombe Home in Calgary.**  Sister Mary Anastase spent the first seven years of her religious life caring for the sick, visiting the needy, and preparing meals at Sisters of Providence centres in Quebec. Then, in 1900, with three other Sisters of Providence (Mathias, Gregoire, and Bois), she was sent to the St. Henry mission at Fort Vermillion. The group spent a month travelling from Montreal to Edmonton, then faced a tortuous, 660-mile trek, by wagon and barge, to Fort Vermillion, where they opened a boarding school for aboriginal children. The Oblate Fathers ran a farm on the mission, and the Sisters were needed to educate and care for the children.

Sister Mary Anastase was 35 years old when she arrived at Fort Vermilion, and she served in the area for 25 years before she was called to the Lacombe Home in 1911 to care for Father Lacombe. She died at Lacombe Home in 1933.

## Louise Crummy McKinney 1868-1931

 **The Alberta provincial election of 1917 was the first in which women, recently enfranchised, could vote. It was also the first in which a woman was elected to a legislative seat. Louise McKinney, destined to be one of Alberta's Famous 5, was the woman. She was elected as an independent representative for Claresholm constituency, a position she held until 1921. Roberta MacAdams was second, winning an overseas vote a few months after Louise.**

A former schoolteacher, Louise came with her husband to homestead in Alberta in 1903. She became involved in a variety of social and political activities. She was a member of the Non-Partisan League, a progenitor of the United Farmers of Alberta, that advocated public ownership of grain elevators and flour mills. A strong member of the Methodist Church, she was the only woman to sign the Basis of Union for the United Church of Canada.

Louise was most involved with the temperance movement. She was a founder of the local Women's Christian Temperance Union (WCTU). Her first public activity was organizing for her local WCTU, and by her death in 1931 she was vice-president of the world organization.

# Emily Ferguson Murphy  1868-1933

**Emily Murphy was a champion of women's rights, a crusader for social reform for more than 25 years, and a respected author, writing under the pen name of 'Janey Canuck.' Today she is probably best remembered as leader of the Famous 5.**

Together with Irene Parlby, Louise McKinney, Nellie McClung, and Henrietta Edwards, Emily petitioned the Supreme Court of Canada for an interpretation of the clause of the British North America Act that prescribed membership in the Senate as being restricted to 'persons.' The group wanted it determined that women were persons in the eyes of the law. In 1928 the Supreme Court ruled against the women. Undaunted, the Famous 5 got the government to take the case to the Privy Council in London, the highest court in the British Empire. The council ruled in their favour, thus establishing women's legal status as persons. The decision was seen as a momentous step forward for women.

Emily Murphy, who had laboured long and at great personal expense, said, "It should be made clear that we are not considering the pronouncement of the Privy Council as standing for a sex victory but rather as one which will now permit our saying 'we' instead of 'you' in all affairs of state."

# Irene Marryat Parlby  1868-1965

**In 1897, Irene Parlby gave up a comfortable privileged life in England to live in a log house in Alberta, where she did much to improve community life.**

She was to say of this period, in a radio broadcast, "First of all, I think, came the exhilarating feeling of living where the world was really young, where there were no people crowding in on you with their miserable, silly little conventions and pettinesses and prejudices, and all the other barnacles people grow when they congregate together in a community."

Irene, however, did not allow the exhilarating aspects of her new life to blind her to the need for reforms in the conditions of rural women. She became the champion of Alberta's farm women and devoted a great deal of energy to improving their lot. She was the first president of the United Farm Women of Alberta, a post she held for three years. In 1921, she entered politics and served as a member of the legislative assembly in the United Farmers of Alberta government. She represented the Lacombe constituency for 14 years. During this time she was minister without portfolio for health and welfare. Irene Parlby is best remembered now as one of Alberta's Famous 5.

# Abigail Edith Blow Condell  1869-1962

**In October, 1962, Edmontonians learned that a Mrs. Condell had left a bequest of $560,000 for the building of an art gallery. The news was electrifying. But who was Mrs. Condell?**

A citizen of Edmonton for over half a centruy, Abigail Blow Condell had been known in music circles but few people knew of her interest in visual art. Abigail studied music at the Canadian College of Music in Ottawa, becoming an accomplished singer and pianist. She was a church organist and choir leader when she married Dr.William N. Condell in 1900. They moved to Edmonton in 1906.

Abigail became an active member of the Women's Musical Club and in 1911 she won the Alberta Musical Festival Medal in Sight Singing. After her husband died, Abigail led a very quiet, frugal life. She invested the money left her by her husband and greatly increased the estate. The Condells' son, Arthur, born in 1905, had died at the age of five, and Abigail had in mind that the art gallery would be a memorial to Arthur. She wanted it to be a cultural asset to Edmonton and all of Alberta. In April, 1969, the Arthur Blow Condell Memorial Building was officially opened.

# Isobel Noble  (born 1869)

**Isobel Noble, first provincial president of the Women's Institutes (WI), had such a capacity to work hard, one man said of her: "She could do the work of two good men!"**

Born in Illinois, Isobel had an unusual education for her day, graduating from the State University of Illinois. She did further study at Cambridge, Yale, and Boston universities. She was supervisor of physical education instruction in the Hartford public schools in Connecticut for five years. With her brother, Tom, she came to Alberta in 1908 from Wichita, Kansas and settled at Daysland, farming there more than 20 years.

An active member of the local WI, Isobel served as provincial president for eight years, and during that time visited every one of the 300 branches in Alberta. She later became supervisor of the newly-organized Alberta WI Girls' Clubs. Isobel and Tom returned to Kansas in 1931, with Isobel becoming active in the League of Womens' Voters and travelling extensively in Africa and the Holy Land. She returned to Alberta in 1959 to celebrate the 50th anniversary of the Women's Institute. She and Marion Rogers maintained an active correspondence for years, sharing news of the women's causes.

# Mildred Lewis Ware 1871-1905

**Mildred Lewis married John Ware, an ex-slave, helped him run a large ranch, and raised their five children. She packed a lot of living into a short span, dying young of pneumonia**

Born in Toronto in 1871, she moved to Alberta in her late teens. There she met John and married him in 1892. Ware had worked for the Bar U and the Quorn Ranches and was well-known for his skill with horses. He already had a ranch on the headwaters of the Sheep River, running 200 head of cattle, when they married. The Wares moved to a new ranch in the Rosebud area in 1902, but their first home was destroyed by the flooding of the Red Deer River. The family barely escaped in the night. Mildred and John prospered though, and their herd increased to 1,000 head. Mildred did the bookkeeping for the ranch and taught her family to read and write. The children went to Blairmore for school, staying with Mildred's mother.

In 1905 Mildred died of pneumonia. When John died shortly after, the Ware children were raised by their grandmother. The Wares' Rosebud log house is now at Dinosaur Park, preserved as a tribute to one of Alberta's noteworthy ranching families.

# Mary McIsaac (born 1873)

**It's a good thing that Mary McIsaac was such a good organizer. First, she consolidated the systems of Edmonton's first school of nursing at what eventually became the Royal Alexandra Hospital. Then she got busy and whipped newly organized chapters of the Women's Institutes (WI) into shape.**

A Cape Breton Islander and graduate of Toronto General Hospital, she came west in 1906 to be the superintendent of what was then called the Boyle Street Hospital, a public non-sectarian hospital opened in 1900. A wooden building that could accommodate 25 patients, the hospital depended on wood and coal stoves for warmth. Stoking those stoves was part of the nurses' jobs. However, thanks to Mary, the nursing curriculum became as important as keeping the place warm.

In 1914, she transferred her health training and organizational skills to the WI, sending out educational material on nutrition, health, homemaking, and childcare to far-flung WI chapters, first in Alberta and then across Canada. Her particular talent lay in recognizing leadership potential and encouraging it. She'd be called a mentor nowadays. From Alberta, she moved to New York State where she continued in public service.

# Margaret Birch Lewis  1873-1941

**When Margaret Birch Lewis came to Calgary from England in 1912, she was already an old-timer in the field of women's rights.**

She was a life member of the Pioneer Clubs, a British suffrage group, and had been active in the Women's Social and Political Union of England. In 1913, she celebrated her 40th birthday, gave birth to her fourth child, and organized a women's suffrage movement. She also became a charter member of the Women's Institute.

When her husband Arthur, who supported her reform activities, was killed in action in 1916, she was left with four young children to raise on a small pension. The next year she was appointed a factory inspector under the new Alberta Factories Act, crossing the province to inspect women's working conditions and to ensure that proper safety and health conditions were met. She also played a leading role in the inquiries which led to the passing of the Alberta Minimum Wage Act for women in 1922. In the early days, Margaret's children travelled everywhere with her. She retired in 1934, after 17 years with the Bureau of Labour.

# Nellie Mooney McClung  1873-1951

**She didn't learn to read until she was 10 and received only six years of formal education, yet Nellie McClung grew up to be a famous author and an articulate advocate for women's rights.**

In 1914, after several volatile years fighting for women's suffrage in Manitoba, she came to Alberta. She continued to play a major role in the campaign that led in 1916 to the vote for women in Manitoba, Alberta, and Saskatchewan. Nellie wrote many of her popular books while in Alberta. She served in the provincial legislature as Liberal member of the legislative assembly for Edmonton, 1921 to 1926. She promoted improved conditions for women and children, old age pensions, mothers' allowances, public health care, and free medical and dental treatment in schools. She was a forceful spokesperson for prohibition; her determined stand against liquor led to her defeat at the polls.

Nellie continued to struggle for women's rights and in 1929 was one of the five Alberta women lobbying to have Canadian women declared 'persons' eligible to sit in the Senate. When asked if she thought women really wanted to sit in the Senate, Nellie said, "After standing over hot stoves and washtubs for all these years, you would think they would be glad to sit anywhere."

# Mary Owen Conquest, O.B.E.  1873-1955

**In the early days of Alberta radio the voice of Mary Conquest, 'The Red Cross Lady,' was familiar to listeners. An informal compilation of Red Cross news, her program was a success from the beginning and on the air for 25 years, despite Mary's own health problems.**

Mary volunteered for the Red Cross Society of Alberta before she became publicity director in 1922. Hired full-time, she travelled provincially, wrote newspaper articles, and made posters, floats, and special displays. When her husband became publisher of the *Athabasca Echo* in 1929, Mary moved to Athabasca and travelled by bus to make her broadcasts. On almost every trip she took along children in need of health care or dental work.

In the early 1930s, Mary had to have her left arm amputated because of Renaud's disease. She returned to her broadcasts, but in 1937 her left leg was amputated. Although she was convalescent for several years, she still did three broadcasts a week, doing her own preparation and script writing. Mary was named a member of the Order of the British Empire in 1942, and until her death in 1955 worked to improve conditions for the handicapped.

# Sister Ignace d'Antioche  1874-1945

**Sister Ignace d'Antioche (Elise Anna Rouleau) was another of the Providence Sisters from Montreal who came to northern Alberta to work with aboriginal children. She was the first teacher at St. Augustine's mission school in Peace River.**

Only 24 when she arrived in Peace River in 1898, Sister Ignace d'Antioche was to spend the next seven years teaching there and watching the boarding school grow from 21 pupils to 59, all either members of the Cree and Beaver tribes, or Metis. Recognizing the students' needs, she added manual and domestic arts to the curriculum, which already included: reading, literature, grammar, geography, penmanship, number work, nature study, hygiene, calisthenics, cooking, sewing and religion. The Sisters and their pupils were housed together in the second-floor dormitory of the two-storey school. The Sisters were also responsible for clothing and nursing the pupils, and Sister Ignace d'Antioche was sacristan, seamstress, and secretary as well.

Sister Ignace d'Antioche later taught in Grouard, Cluny, and New Westminster, spending 30 years in all as a teacher before moving to a hospital position, where she spent the rest of her life doing lighter duties.

# Maude Cowling Bowman 1875-1944

**Founding director of the Edmonton Art Club, Maude Bowman worked without pay for 20 years to keep the dream of a community public art centre alive. With other dedicated volunteers, she was responsible for the birth of the Edmonton Art Gallery.**

A native of Cornwall, England, Maude moved with her family to Canada and married David Bowman in Berlin (now Kitchener), Ontario. They settled in Edmonton and raised five children, and Maude became an early supporter of cultural life in the city. In 1923, when the Edmonton Art Club was formed, she became its first president and director. During the club's difficult early years, she nurtured it from exhibition space on a wall of the library through its later moves into the Macdonald Hotel and the Civic Block.

Besides supporting art exhibits for the city, Maude was instrumental in bringing noted musicians to Edmonton for concerts. She served many years with the Music Festival Society and the Women's Musical Club, opening her home for recitals and meet-the-artist receptions. When she died in 1944, she was recognized for her outstanding contribution to the artistic life of her community.

# CHAPTER 2: 1876-1900

# Sister Ambrose Lenkewich  1876-1953

**When Sister Ambrose Marcella Lenkewich arrived in Edmonton from the Ukraine in 1902, she was the leader of a group of four Sisters Servants of Mary Immaculate, the first missionaries to be sent abroad by that Order.**

The Sisters came to Canada to serve among the Ukrainian immigrants settling in Edmonton and in the Willingdon-Mundare area. The immigrants were longing for priests and church services in their own faith. Father Lacombe arranged for the group to stay with the Grey Nuns and to learn English at the Ruthenian Young Ladies Club in Edmonton.

Within a year, the Sisters moved to a mission just started at Beaver Lake (Mundare); they began their religious duties and helped build up the farm there. Sister Ambrose, the Superior, was a trained nurse with an impressive knowledge of herbs. She offered comfort and reassurance in those early years to sick and dying Ukrainians as she nursed them with familiar medications, talked to them in their language, and repeated the prayers of their faith. Under her strong leadership from 1902 to 1926, other Canadian missions were formed, as well as a school and a children's home.

# Sarah 'Ailie' Lendrum Brick  1877-1947

**Two days after high-spirited Ailie Lendrum, 19, married Fred Brick, an independent fur trader, she set out on the difficult 700-mile journey to Fort Vermilion. It was a trip the couple would make every spring and every fall for the next 11 years.**

Carting supplies for the coming year, they travelled up the Athabasca and Lesser Slave rivers, sailed 90 miles across Lesser Slave Lake (a dangerous, storm-fraught trip in which they lost a canoe-load of precious supplies), portaged 100 miles in wagons drawn by unbroken horses, and came at last to the Peace River. Then they constructed a 100-foot raft and, cooking, sleeping, and eating on board, floated in unstable fashion, with animals and baggage, 300 miles down river to the fort.

At the fort, Ailie lived the life of a frontier wife. With childhood chores done mostly outdoors, she knew little of housekeeping. "I had never made a loaf of bread, a cake, or a pie in my life. But my husband had batched it for some time and was very patient with me." Three of her four children were born at Fort Vermilion. A Metis midwife attended, and Ailie said, "I shall never forget (her) as she helped and comforted me . . . 700 miles from doctor or nurse."

# Alice Curtis 1877-1957

**A founder of the home and school movement in Alberta, Alice Curtis worked for more than 40 years to forge links between parents and educators.**

A graduate of the Ottawa Normal School, Alice accompanied her husband to Alberta in 1903 and began raising a family of three girls. In 1914, she became the first president of a Mothers' Club at Connaught School, the first such club in the West. She saw the potential for such organizations to improve communication between home and school and helped organize clubs at other schools, sometimes against the opposition of teachers.

When her husband died in 1921, Alice returned to teaching to support her family. She continued to work establishing co-operative home and school organizations and played a lead role when the Calgary Home and School Federation was born in 1926. During the Depression, her groups provided radios, library books, and art supplies to the impoverished school system. Alice served as first secretary of the Alberta Home and School Association and secretary-treasurer of the national organization, which awarded her a life membership in 1951. An elementary school in Calgary's Acadia district was named in her honour in 1964.

# Jean McWilliam McDonald 1877-1969

**Jean McWilliam had been in the work force since she was 11 years old, and she was to become one of Calgary's more colourful fighters for social reform.**

Jean came to the city with two small children after a marriage breakdown and an unsuccessful homesteading venture. Following a series of menial jobs, she opened a boarding house, around 1911. She also worked as matron for the police department. Without much formal education, Jean became an outspoken and energetic supporter of causes that ranged through old age pensions, assistance for the poor, unsatisfactory hospital conditions, licensing of chiropractors, plight of local aboriginals, and the starvation wages of women factory workers.

When they locked horns at a public meeting over the inadequacy of allowances for soldiers' wives, R.B. Bennett reprimanded Jean for haranguing him and threatened to charge her with slander. He probably expected her to be cowed by his presence, but he had underestimated the spirit of the woman confronting him. "I looked him square in the eye and answered, 'Mr. Bennett, to the rest of the women of Calgary you may be God Almighty, but to me you are just plain R.B. Bennett, and you do not frighten me one bit!' "

# Annie Gale  1877-1970

**Mouldy carrots and the high cost of housing in Calgary in 1912 helped transform a conservative immigrant housewife into a determined suffragette.**

When Annie and William Gale emigrated from England to Canada, they arrived in the middle of an economic boom. Fresh, often inferior, vegetables were so expensive that Annie asked why. It turned out that local storekeepers brought produce from British Columbia on contract; they couldn't use locally grown produce. Annie couldn't believe it – or what immigrant families were forced to pay for a home. Then she heard that livestock on isolated farms got more medical attention than pregnant women. That did it. Over the next few years, she organized the Consumers League, the Vacant Lots Garden Club, the Free Hospitals League, and the Women's Ratepayers Association. She encouraged women to take part in municipal politics, not as partisan politicians, but as people guided by the righteousness and justice of each issue.

In 1917, she was elected to Calgary city council, the first woman alderman in the British Empire. Annie served as acting mayor on occasion, again a first for a woman. In 1924, she was elected to the school board.

# Mary Isabel Ross Pinkham, O.B.E.   1878-1964

**Mary Pinkham followed her parents' example and devoted her life to church and community efforts.**

She was born in Winnipeg in 1878 and came to Calgary in 1889 with her parents, Bishop and Mrs. W. C. Pinkham. A founder of the Alberta Division of the Canadian Red Cross Society, she covered the province during World War I, organizing Red Cross branches and devoting 50 years of service to the organization.

Mary was attached to many women's organizations in Calgary: those at Pro-Cathedral of the Redeemer, the Women's Hospital Aid Society, and the Imperial Order of Daughters of the Empire. For a number of years, she was bursar of St. Hilda's College for girls, a school founded by her father. She was proud of having been presented with life memberships in both the Diocesan and Dominion Boards of the Women's Auxiliary. Among many honours, Mary received the Jubilee medal for community service and was decorated with the Order of the British Empire in 1935. She was honoured with two of three possible Red Cross awards in Canada, and was also elected an Honourary Associate of the Order of St John of Jerusalem in England.

# Dora Brock Brainard 1878-1967

**Dora Brock Brainard arrived in Peace River Country just in time to celebrate her 40th birthday and set up a stopping place for travellers on the Grand Prairie-Pouce Coupe Trail.**

Dora came to join her husband, Lee, at Sinclair Lake, half-way point on the trail. While Lee homesteaded, 'Ma' Brainard and her daughter served home-cooked meals to settlers, teamsters, Northwest Mounted Police, and commercial travellers. They operated from abandoned buildings beside the lake and then from a log house Lee built.

Sometimes 20 teams and teamsters put up at Ma Brainard's, with 40 or 50 eating her famous chicken dinners. The charge: fifty cents for all you could eat. Inability to pay didn't mean you went hungry at Ma's. Legend has it that she gave away as many meals as she sold. Because she used a thousand birds a season, Ma raised her own chickens. She always had 'one in the pan, one ready to put in the pan, and some handy at the door ready for the axe.' Dora gave hot meals and shelter to travellers for almost 50 years, and treated all with the same warmth and good humour. "I never put on for anybody, I serve them all the same," she said.

# Mildred Dobbs 1878-1974

**In 1911 Mildred Dobbs, an English nurse visiting her brother in Lethbridge, fell in love with the West she described as "a little bit of heaven." She became a nurse at the local isolation hospital, a draughty old building three miles from town. Retiring in 1951 at age 74, Mildred was especially proud of two things: her good health (she had taken only five days sick leave in 38 years) and her record of no cross-infections among her patients.**

Mildred was on duty 24 hours a day. Working with an erratic water supply and six fires to heat the building in winter – sometimes with housekeeping help, sometimes with none – she single-handedly nursed patients through the contagious diseases of the day. She fought scarlet fever, measles, typhoid, smallpox, and polio. Conditions in the old house were primitive: beds were folding cots made up with discarded police blankets; her request, after 10 years, that a pot and tablecloth be replaced got a reply: "There were two tablecloths when we opened. What happened to the other one?" Life as an isolation nurse was lonely. Mildred almost never left the hospital. There was the chance of spreading infection, and there was no one to replace her.

# Julia 'Juey' Scott Lawrence   1879-1974

As a seven-year-old, Julia 'Juey' Scott Lawrence first saw Fort Vermilion when her father, Rev. Malcolm Scott, brought the family from Winnipeg to live at St. Luke's Mission.

    She was 'sent out' for schooling at St. John's Ladies College, Red River. She returned to Fort Vermilion to teach at the mission and later married Sheridan Lawrence, farmer and trader. They established the Ranch at Stoney Point, developing it extensively during their residence of over half a century.

    Juey was tiny, resourceful, and determined her children would not be sent out for schooling. So she developed a school on her own, Lawrence Point school, the first north of Peace River village. Mother of 15 children, she boarded children and teachers in the early years to have the required number of pupils for a school. Her work included serving this large household, preserving meat, sewing, raising a big garden, doing bookkeeping, and tanning furs and skins. With no doctor in the area, Juey also filled in for medical emergencies. She nursed her husband and all 15 of the children through small pox. When almost 60, she flew north to join her husband for his last winter of trading at his posts at Hay River and Hay Lakes.

# Emma Mary Johnstone, O.B.E.   1879-1975

Emma Johnstone's willingness to accept challenges made her a determined fighter for better health facilities, 'flying doctors,' and air ambulance services. She served as a pioneer doctor in northern Alberta for more than 30 years.

    At age five, Emma promised her dying mother that she would never do a thing because it was nice or because she liked it, but because it was right. At age fifteen she moved to England from India, after her father too died. With the courage she had as a child, she announced that she intended to study medicine. Overcoming opposition from family and medical circles, she graduated in 1910. Later, again after opposition, she obtained a diploma in psychological medicine from Cambridge.

    By 1927, Emma needed a break from work in mental institutions. She answered a medical journal ad and accepted a job in northern Alberta. At age 47 and in poor health, she became the first woman district doctor first at Jarvie, Wanham, and then Wandering River. Her practice lasted 30 years, although she returned to England during World War II as medical officer at a London mobile aid unit. Emma was named a member of the Order of the British Empire.

# Grace Martin McEachern  1879-1988

**Grace Martin was the first teacher in the Ellerslie district, just south of Edmonton; she lived to see an Edmonton school named in her honour 50 years later.**

Born in North Dakota, Grace moved to Edmonton with her parents and 10 brothers and sisters in 1899. After her father died, she went to Normal School in Regina, then the capital of the North West Territories. Her first teaching job began at the new Frank Oliver School in the Ellerslie district early in 1902. While she boarded there during the week, she went home to Edmonton to help her mother on weekends. Sometimes, engineers on the local train would give her a lift in the engine to save her the walk. With photography as a hobby, Grace kept an unusual photographic record of her pupils.

In 1903 Grace moved to the Leduc school, where she met her husband, Donald McEachern, the principal. As wife, mother of one, and homemaker, she retained her interest in education and developed a special relationship with the pupils of the school named in her honour, the Grace Martin Elementary School. A widow since 1946, Grace died in 1988 at age 108.

# Margaret Haskins Greenham  1880-1960

**Margaret Greenham, founder of the Mountain School of Banff, Alberta, was a vibrant teacher whose sponsorship of the arts helped make Banff internationally recognized as a cultural centre.**

Born Margaret Haskins in Bristol, England, she graduated from Clifton College and studied French in Paris for two years before emigrating in 1908. She became a teacher at Havergal College, Toronto, where she taught English and was active in the Coverley literary society and amateur theatrical productions. In 1915, she married a teacher, Henry Warren Greenham, and the couple moved west to Pine Lake, Alberta.

In 1919, they settled in Banff and established a private school which soon began drawing pupils from around the world. In 1923, Margaret organized the Banff Literary and Dramatic Society. She founded a children's dramatic group, Merry Go Round Theatre, which she directed until ill-health forced her retirement in 1959. She was instrumental in the establishment of the Banff community library, and was a regular reviewer of books for the *Crag and Canyon* newspaper until her death. The Banff Centre's Margaret Greenham Theatre was named in recognition of her energetic contributions to the arts.

# Maude Keen Riley   1880-1962

**Maude Riley's motivation, courage, and determination led her into a long life of service to Calgary and Alberta. Sometimes referred to as a tyrant, she was also was known as a colourful figure who got things done.**

Following a serious illness as a young mother, Maude made a covenant – if she lived, she would devote her life to mothers and children. Born and educated in Ontario, Maude Keen came to Calgary to teach in 1904. In 1907 she married Harold W. Riley and became the mother of three children. In 1918, she helped found the Alberta Council on Child and Family Welfare and became president in 1922/1923, remaining in the post for 39 years.

While council president, Maude was a member of many kindred organizations – usually at the executive level. She was often a step or two ahead of legislators in many of the things she advocated, such as a clean bill of health for both people obtaining a marriage license, pasteurization of milk, family allowances, free hospitalization for maternity cases, and better nutrition for school children. In 1937 she received the King George VI Coronation Medal, and in 1946 she was the first woman named Calgary Citizen of the Year.

# Allison Campbell Procter, O.B.E.   1880-1964

**Though she worked hard for many social causes, Allison Procter is best known for her outstanding service with the Canadian Red Cross Society during World War II, mobilizing and directing women volunteers across northern Alberta.**

Volunteers were organized into working units, and materials distributed to them were made into clothing and bandages. Finished articles were carefully inspected at the main office in Edmonton, and, if they met the high standards of the Red Cross, were shipped overseas. Allison supervised every aspect of the operation and was rewarded with remarkable enthusiasm and co-operation from the branches under her jurisdiction. More than one million items were shipped from her depot in Edmonton. Allison lost both her sons in the war, and despite her sorrow, continued with the Red Cross through the post-war period. She was named to the Order of the British Empire for her war work.

Allison came to Alberta in 1911 with her husband, Richard Procter, a doctor. An avid collector of art objects and handicrafts, she became especially interested in Ukrainian textile and metal work. In 1963 she donated more than a hundred of her treasured weavings to the Provincial Museum.

# Marie-Anne Leblanc Gravel  1880-1979

**Marie-Anne Gravel personifies the courage and
determination of prairie women, withstanding
tragedy to contribute to life in her community.**
Arriving from Quebec in 1912, a widow with
two small children, she was the first woman to file a
claim or live on a homestead in the Donnelly area. Soon
after she arrived, both her children died, victims of
contaminated water. Marie-Anne persisted through this
and through the other trials that homesteading presented.
She felled trees and worked the land. With her second
husband, Eugene Gravel, she built an immigration hall
for new settlers to the area. In the great influenza

epidemic of 1918 and a subsequent smallpox epidemic, the hall became an
isolation ward, with Marie-Anne acting as nurse and attending the sick. The
hall, which evolved into the Hotel Gravel, was an important social centre for the
growing community, a favourite gathering place for holidays and celebrations.
Surviving her husband, and their son, a Royal Canadian Air Force pilot
killed in World War II, Marie-Anne continued many pursuits with characteristic
energy and generosity. At 95, she and her sister were knitting 100 pairs of
mittens a year for the needy. Marie-Anne died in 1979 at almost 100.

# Jessie Mary 'Chappie' Chapman  1880-1981

**With cheerfulness and dedication, Jessie Mary
'Chappie' Chapman helped thousands of Calgary
passengers: the blind, the sick, the elderly, the lost,
children travelling alone, people stranded without
funds, immigrants, service families during the war,
refugees, war brides, and hungry infants soothed by a
special gadget she used to warm their bottles.**
Born and raised in London, England, Chappie
was almost 50 when she came to Calgary in 1929.
Almost immediately she began working for the Young
Women's Christian Association (YWCA) at their travel-
ler's aid booth in the Canadian Pacific station. Chappie once described her work
as "emergency service to all those in need," and she set no limits to her efforts.
She welcomed all who passed through the station, including Royal visitors in
1939. In 1946, nearly 5,000 people were helped by the service.
Passenger numbers decreased, and Chappie was able to operate the aid
booth alone in 1966 and 1967, when she was in her 80s. She was chosen one of
14 YWCA national Women of the Century in 1967 and retired soon after. On
her 100th birthday in 1980, friends brought Chappie a bouquet of 100 yellow
roses, honouring her remarkable contribution to Calgary's development.

# Jane Megarry  1881-1958

**Jane Megarry is remembered with honour on the Blackfoot and Blood Reserves of southern Alberta, where she served from 1914 until 1937 as a nursing missionary at Anglican residential schools.**

Born in Ireland, she arrived in Canada at the age of 30 hoping to become a medical missionary in the west. In 1914, she became nurse in charge of the Blackfoot Indian Hospital at Gleichen, Alberta, She found most patients were suffering from tuberculosis. In order to care for them better, she learned the Blackfoot language.

In 1920, she furthered her nursing training at the Galt Hospital, Lethbridge. On graduation in 1923, she became head matron of St. Paul's Residential School on the Blood Reserve near Fort Macleod. She oversaw the move from the old school to a new site near Cardston in 1924, and served as matron there until 1937. During the summers, she trained children in first aid at a holiday camp at Waterton Lake. Jane was made an honourary member of the Blood Tribe and given the name On-ataki, which translates as "good woman." She was also honoured when named by King George V as a serving sister to the Order of St. John of Jerusalem.

# Roberta Catherine MacAdams Price  1881-1959

**Tenacity must have been one of Roberta MacAdams Price's special qualities. One of the first two women elected in 1917 to a British Commonwealth legislature, after Louise McKinney, she won her seat while serving overseas.**

She went on to introduce a bill to incorporate the War Veteran's Next-of-Kin Association. This made her the first woman to introduce a piece of legislation in any legislature in the Commonwealth.

Born into a family of newspaper people, Roberta learned early to make her own choices. After two years' training in domestic science at the Macdonald Institute, Guelph, she came to explore opportunities in Alberta. She was hired to conduct short courses for farm women, the forerunner of the province's District Home Economists' program. Travelling on a demonstration train, she spoke on foods and cookery. In 1912 she was superintendent of domestic science in Edmonton public schools, where she won a battle to teach cooking in class. In 1916, she was commissioned a lieutenant in the Canadian Army Medical Corps, serving at an English hospital. After the War, the Soldier Settlement Board named Roberta a counsellor for war brides. She later married Harry Price, and raised a son.

# Hughena Elliott McCorquodale  1881-1961

The "dean of prairie newspaperwomen" and a "Western institution" were two of the terms other writers used to describe Hughena Elliott 'Corky' McCorquodale when she died in 1961. She had been editor of the *High River Times* for years and on the paper's staff for almost 30.

Originally trained as a teacher, Hughena came to Alberta in 1906. She married Alexander McCorquodale in 1908 and moved to High River. It was while raising her family of three sons that she began to write. First she freelanced articles to magazines, and then in 1927 she joined the Times. She stayed on staff until 1956, when a community tea in her honour drew 600 people to the High River Memorial Centre.

Corky was known for her sense of humour and her love for the people she wrote about. She was a vice-president of the local chapter of the Canadian Women's Press Club and known to be particularly helpful to young writers. The Stoney honoured her with the name 'Eagle Woman' for her efforts to help them obtain an Eden Valley reserve in the early 1940s.

# Olive Dolly Ross  1881-1970

Dolly Ross, daughter of early Edmonton pioneers, was a girl with a strong streak of independence. Educated in Edmonton, she studied business and worked for the firm of Emery and Beck as a legal secretary for six years. Deciding the work was joyless and unrewarding, she went to Montreal to train at the Royal Victoria Hospital, becoming the first Edmonton-born woman to graduate as a nurse.

Dolly nursed at the Edmonton Public Hospital on Boyle Street and then did missionary medical work for the Presbyterian Church in Grande Prairie for a year. During World War I, she served as a military nurse in Malta and England. After Armistice she was posted to the military hospital at Esquimalt, British Columbia for four years.

In 1926 the Women's Missionary Society asked her to run a medical mission at Fort McMurray. Turning an old log dance hall into a residence, office, and three-bed hospital, she provided medical services to people in the area until 1934. Returning to Edmonton she nursed at her old hospital, renamed the Royal Alexandra, until she retired.

# Annie Siddall Gaetz  1881-1972

**Annie Siddall Gaetz is honoured in Red Deer for her contributions as a teacher, author, and preserver of the city's pioneer heritage.**

Born and raised in Cumberland County, Nova Scotia, Annie Siddall came west in 1903 to become the teacher at Mound Lake school (Ardley) east of Red Deer. The only equipment provided was blackboard and some chalk. In 1904, she married Frederick Warren Gaetz, son of Dr. Leonard and Caroline Gaetz who had homesteaded in 1884 on the site of the future city. Together Annie and Fred raised a family of four children, and Annie became deeply involved in community activities in the growing village. A long-serving Sunday School teacher and president of the Womens' Christian Temperance Union, Annie also earned life memberships in the United Church Women's Missionary Society and the Canadian Red Cross.

In 1948, she published a local history, *The Park Country*, and followed it with *Trails of Yesterday* and an historical narrative of the Gaetz family, *Footprints*. She was instrumental in the compilation of Red Deer's community history, *Book of Memories,* and in the founding of the Red Deer Archives Committee, to which she donated significant material.

# Lucy Lowe Bagnall  1882-1969

**When her Baptist minister husband was killed in a car accident in 1920, Lucy Lowe Bagnall saw her duty and did it. She completed the temperance lectures that he had planned for southern Alberta, then she taught school to support their two young children.**

Lucy had already faced some challenges as a missionary's wife. Muskeg, for one thing, never ending swamps that made their horse-and-buggy trip to their first charge in the Peace River country nearly impossible. But she had grit, part of her Nova Scotia legacy, and helped her husband establish a new church at Clairmont, now near Grande Prairie. They also served the pastorates of Nelson, British Columbia, and Medicine Hat.

While teaching for 20 years at Western Canada High School in Calgary, Lucy added two more degrees to her name, a master's in arts and a master's in education from the University of Alberta. Her first degrees were from Nova Scotia's Acadia University. In 1938 they remembered her with an honourary doctorate. Ever faithful to the Baptist Church, Lucy taught Sunday School regularly, belonged to the Women's Missionary Society, and wrote the history of Calgary's First Baptist Church on the occasions of its 60th and 75 anniversaries.

# Marion Smyth Rogers  1882-1976

**Marion Smyth Rogers believed in the 'hands on' approach to getting things done. When branches of the Women's Institute (WI) were organized throughout Alberta, from 1916 on, Marion travelled by train, wagon, and even jigger, to encourage these new forums where women of all creeds could meet as homemakers and mothers.**

Marion served the provincial and federal WI groups for many years, but her satisfaction came from the friendships nurtured in WI chapters. During the war years, Alberta WI chapters concentrated on helping the Merchant Navy, with Marion checking and packing ditty bags in Navy League quarters. Marion served as corresponding secretary and recording secretary for the Federated Women's Institutes of Canada, later writing a history of the federation up to 1935.

Also active in school affairs, Marion was a member of the Fort Saskatchewan school board for 15 years. She was secretary-treasurer of the Alberta School Trustees' Association for 23 years and edited their magazine. She also served on the Salvation Army advisory board for 20 years. In 1967, Marion was awarded a Canada Confederation Medal.

# Donalda James Dickie  1883-1972

**Donalda Dickie was a scholar, author, and a leading educator in Alberta. An ex-student once said, "She made the business of learning an adventure."**

On the staff of the Alberta Normal Schools, Calgary, Camrose, and Edmonton, from 1912 to 1944, Donalda wrote more than 50 books, including professional manuals, school readers, children's books, geography books, and a long series of history books. Perhaps her finest achievement and most ambitious project was *The Great Adventure*, her history of Canada for use in junior high schools, for which she received the Governor-General's Award for Juvenile Literature for 1950.

Donalda received her early education in Ontario and took her teacher's training at Regina Normal. She obtained her master's degree in 1910 from Queen's University and then did post graduate work at Columbia and Oxford. The latter did not yet grant degrees to women, so she earned her doctorate in history from the University of Toronto in 1910 and received an honourary doctorate of laws there in 1952. In 1961 she was the third woman to be made an honourary member of the Alberta Teachers' Association. She was also interested in the Women's Press Club and the Alberta Authors Association.

# Annie Mabel McLeod  1884-1950

**Mabel McLeod endured the hardship of losing her mother when she was young. This was not the only hardship Mabel would confront in her lifetime. As a pioneer nurse she would face many more.**

Mabel graduated from the Lady Stanley Institute for Trained Nurses in Ottawa in 1911. She moved to Calgary via California in 1915, and before long was matron of both the High River hospital and the nurses' training school. In the 1930s she was matron of the Vulcan hospital. Hearing about the injuries of the oilfield workers and the lack of nearby medical aid, Mabel decided to start a hospital at Turner Valley. She persuaded Cora Stayffer Burke to help her. In 1940 they opened a six-bed hospital in an abandoned cookhouse and lived in the dug-out basement for the first six months.

With energy, ingenuity, and resourcefulness the two co-founders and co-matrons of Oilfields Hospital added beds and a maternity wing. When Mabel died, there was a twenty-four bed hospital in operation. Mabel's services as a pioneer nurse were recognized in 1935 when she received the King George V Silver Jubilee Medal.

# Annie M. Jackson

**Annie Jackson made history on June 21, 1913, when she was sworn in as Alberta's – and perhaps Canada's – first full-time female police officer. Appointed a constable with the Edmonton Police Department, she was given the special responsibility of upholding the morals and manners of the young women of the city.**

Annie served with the police force until 1916, and was credited, according to a 1913 report in the London *Daily Mirror*, with having "reduced the tendency of girls to indulge in hoydenish conduct on the streets" as she went about her "her special duty to look after the morals and manners of Edmonton's young girls."

Annie was not the first Alberta woman to crack the all-male police force, however. A colleague, Emma Robinson, had been working with the police on an on-call basis since 1900, assisting them in cases involving missing women or females under arrest. When the Edmonton Police Department asked city council to name Emma a constable in 1900, they refused, however. Emma did continue with both the city police and the mounted police, on a part-time basis, until she retired in 1931.

# Johanna Haakstad  1885-1963

**Practical nurse Johanna Haakstad delivered over 3,000 babies in the south Peace River country. Known as 'Aunt Jo' to most everyone in the country, she was dearly loved for her devoted service and kindness to her patients, both big and small.**

Johanna began her nursing career as a travelling nurse. That is, she would walk or ride horseback to the home of the expectant mother and stay with her until the baby came. However, distances and weather in the north made that a dicey proposition. How much better it would be to have a permanent location where the mothers could come in advance and wait for their babies. In 1928, the Women's Institute bought a two-room shack in Sexsmith and set it up as a hospital with Johanna in charge. That worked for awhile, but it was soon too small. Eventually, Johanna bought her own house and set it up as a six-bed maternity home. That worked very well.

In 1948, she and her Maternity Hospital both retired, but her 3,000 children – and especially their mothers – couldn't let Aunt Jo go without a certain amount of ceremony. So they had a parade of children. Maybe there weren't 3,000 there, but there were many.

# Rose Owens Wilkinson  1885-1968

**Rose Owens Wilkinson was always known as 'Rosie,' but that doesn't mean she was a frail little flower. Anything but.**

She looked around at Calgary in the 1930s and decided a few things needed changing. So she ran for city council in 1935, won handily, and kept them hopping for the next 19 years. Then in the 1940s, she looked around Alberta and decided a few things needed changing. So she ran for the provincial government as a member of the Social Credit party in 1944, won handily, and kept them hopping for the next 19 years. Always Rosie spoke out on behalf of the 'little guy,' and the little guy rewarded her for her loyalty by giving more votes to her than any other candidate. She regularly topped the polls in both civic and provincial elections. Often she declared, "Legislative bodies, to be representative, should be composed of men and women."

Born in Ireland, trained in nursing in England, Rosie came to Calgary with her husband Frederick Wilkinson in 1927. She set up a physiotherapy clinic and lectured at the Holy Cross School of Nursing. Her expertise was treating infectious diseases, an important aspect of nursing before antibiotics.

# Violet McCully Barss 1885-1971

**For 50 years, Violet Barss – 'Aunt Vi' as she was known to her town – was the primary health care provider for the town of Delia and vicinity. She was also the town's mayor.**

From 1912, when she arrived in the district as a graduate nurse, she voluntarily offered her medical and midwifery skills in the service of her neighbours. For many years, there was no doctor in the area, and the community relied on Violet for emergency care. Born in St. Mary's, Ontario, Violet McCully entered the Allegheny General Hospital Training School, Pittsburgh, Pennsylvania, in 1904 to begin nursing training. She came west to High River in 1911, then joined her brother, Campbell McCully, on his farm in the Delia area in 1912. She married William Barss, a local carpenter and woodworker, in 1913. During the influenza epidemic of 1918, Violet worked selflessly nursing those who fell ill.

Violet was already a local councillor when she was elected mayor of Delia in 1920 and served until 1922, the first woman to hold a mayoralty position in Alberta. Later she was named to the board of governors of the University of Alberta.

# May Hall Laidlaw, C.M. 1885-1976

**May Hall Laidlaw did much to preserve history in Medicine Hat, working hard to establish its museum and recording the stories of early pioneers in the area.**

Born and educated in Manitoba, May attended the Boston Conservatory of Music, where she studied language, voice, and piano. After she married Lorne Laidlaw and moved to Medicine Hat in 1910, she became active in community affairs. After Lorne died in 1946, May became interested in the Historical Society and worked hard to establish the town's first museum. She is credited with much of the work it took to build a new museum and to have it enlarged. May also found time to record the voices of some of the area's pioneers, preserving their stories for future generations.

As well as the museum, May worked for the Young Women's Christian Association, Red Cross, the Dramatic and Operatic societies, St. John's Presbyterian Church, and the development of music and drama in Medicine Hat. May and Lorne had three sons, one of whom died in World War II. In June, 1974, May was appointed a member of the Order of Canada for the contributions she made to the community over more than 60 years.

# Maude Lucas Smart 1886-1963

**Maude Lucas Smart spent 37 years of her life nursing, using good humour, lots of common sense, and an ability to improvise.**

Isabelle Maude Lucas was born and grew up on the Peace Hills Agency Farm just north of Wetaskiwin. Her home was one of five stopping places on the Calgary-Edmonton Trail. Her playmates were the nearby native children, and she learned their language.

After graduation from the Holy Cross Hospital in Calgary in 1914 she nursed at the Wetaskiwin hospital, until leaving for overseas during World War I. Following the war and post-graduate work in New York, Maude was one of four nurses hired by the Department of Indian Affairs to visit all the reservations in the three prairie provinces. At the request of the government she took a course in the treatment of tuberculosis. The needs of the locals were great, but supplies and money were insufficient to carry out her work. She travelled on foot, by horseback, dog team, horse and buggy, and on snowshoes.

After retirement Maude nursed at Grande Prairie, where she met and married Archie Smart in 1945. Archie died in 1960, and Maude spent the last three years of her life in Edmonton.

# Jenny Le Rouge Le Saunier 1886-1971

**Jenny Le Rouge gave up a promising music career when she and her family moved to Alberta, but Edmonton gained an exceptional music teacher.**

Even as a child, Jenny showed unusual musical ability and was already appearing as a guest pianist on concert stages in Europe when her father decided to emigrate to Alberta. They settled in Red Deer eventually, but opportunities were few and far between for a concert pianist there so Jenny began teaching piano. She did get a trip to Ottawa to play at Rideau Hall for Sir Wilfred Laurier and Earl Grey, but that was about the extent of her concert career in Canada.

Instead, she married Charles Le Saunier and moved to Edmonton. There she continued teaching piano for 40 years and gained a reputation as the best teacher of both students and other teachers. In 1952, she was awarded the *Palmes d'officier d'Acadamie* by the Ambassador of France who came to Edmonton especially for the occasion. Her adopted country took its turn in 1966 when the University of Alberta gave her an honourary doctor of laws.

# Winifred Thompson Ross 1886-1974

**Winifred Thompson Ross' vision went beyond Alberta or even Canada. She believed that through the Farm Women's Union of Alberta (FWUA), farm women found a voice in international farm organizations and at the United Nations.**

Winnifred is credited with bringing the FWUA into the Association Country Women of the World (ACWW). She attended ACWW conferences in Edinburg in 1959 and Dublin in 1965. A war widow, Winnifred started farming in 1918 at Millet. From the time she joined the Millet local of the FWUA in 1919, she was interested in raising the standards for rural schooling and promoting adult education. For 24 years she served the FWUA as a provincial leader. She also served on the original committee of the National Farm Forums, the Canadian Research Committee on Practical Education, and the advisory committee to the Schools of Agriculture.

Winnifred was appointed to the board of governors of the University of Alberta in 1948. She was vice-president of the Alberta Council on Child and Welfare. She was a member of the Alberta Health Survey Committee, which led to the development of provincial health units.

# Signe Spokkeli Hills 1886-1988

**When the Town of Camrose honoured its oldest old-timer and first teacher in 1980, Signe Spokkeli Hills was 94 years old.**

Coming to Alberta from Minnesota in 1885, Signe spoke only Norwegian. Her education began in a settler's shack, then in the local school when it was finally built. For high school she had to go to Edmonton. Graduating in 1907, Signe went to Regina to attend Normal School. Classes were held back then in the upstairs 'assembly room' of a high school. Her first school was not quite completed when she began classes, and Signe had to use big pieces of wrapping paper to substitute for blackboards. Her daughter recalls that teaching days were happy ones for her mother: "Among mother's schooldays memories were those of lunches, slates, noisy slate-pencils, the slate rag and its bottle of water, cold mornings, the big stove in the centre of the room, and the day the hail storm broke all the windows."

Signe had a pioneer's approach to the difficulties and hardships of early teaching in Alberta: "Through it all, even when she was boarding in a sod-roofed house which couldn't keep out the rain, Mother remembered most the pioneer cheerfulness, friendliness, and will to succeed."

# Elizabeth Bailey Price  1887-1944

**Elizabeth Bailey Price loved to write, although her first employment was as a schoolteacher in the Olds and later Calgary areas.**

In 1911, she joined the editorial staff of *The Albertan*, serving as women's editor for a number of years. While there, she met and married the sports editor, Joe Price. Elizabeth served as president of the Canadian Women's Press Club in 1932, as well as heading the Calgary and Vancouver branches. Her interest in women's work led to her participation in organizing the Calgary branch of the Women's Institute (WI), in 1918. Almost 20 years later, when WI branches in Canada numbered 2,860, Elizabeth was their representative at the 1936 3rd Triennial International Conference of the Associated Countrywomen of the World, in Washington, DC.

A successful author, Elizabeth wrote *My Seventy Years*, the biography of Mrs. George Black, former Conservative member of parliament for the Yukon. While in Edmonton, she helped produce a book on club women's records. Women's interests remained close to her heart, and she continued her whole life to support progressive causes.

# Dorothy Sheila Marryat  1887-1962

**A famous early radio personality, Sheila Marryat was the first radio secretary and director of programs at CKUA, the University of Alberta (U of A) radio station.**

Born and educated in England, Sheila was the youngest child of Col. and Mrs. E.L. Marryat. She came to Alberta at the age of 16 when her father retired to ranch at Haunted Lakes near Alix. Sheila's older sister, Irene Parlby, became one of Alberta's Famous 5 women who worked to have the British Privy Council declare Canadian women 'persons' under law.

Sheila completed a bachelor of science in agriculture in 1923 at U of A, where she acted with the University Dramatic Club and impressed the university president, Dr. Robert Wallace, with her talent. He invited her to direct the fledgling CKUA. For 12 years, she was program director, dramatist, script writer, on-air hostess, and technician for the station. She formed the CKUA Players, who performed works by Alberta playwrights. Her *Building of Canada* series was picked up by the Canadian Broadcasting Corporation (CBC) and broadcast nationally. In 1938, she became a Winnipeg-based producer for the CBC. She died in retirement in Victoria in 1962.

# Catherine Nichols Gunn  1887-1979

**Catherine Nichols Gunn cared for school children for 30 years as a member of the Calgary Health Department. She had been a nurse overseas in World War I and also worked with tuberculosis (TB) patients.**

Born in Nova Scotia, 'Nichols' trained as a nurse in Seattle and went overseas with the Canadian Army in 1916. After the war ended, she spent a year taking care of French civilians injured in the fighting. By 1922 she had joined the Calgary Health Department, providing care to countless school children in the northern part of the city for the next 30 years. Catherine Nichols Gunn Elementary School was named in her honour because she typified the role of the public health nurse in the school.

Nichols was also a volunteer with the Canadian National Institute for the Blind for 18 years and was a dedicated member of Chalmers Presbyterian Church. The women's group honoured her for her work with new Canadians, the sick, the lonely, and the bereaved. She cared for TB patients for many years, especially those who came back from overseas with the disease.

# Cora Watt Casselman  1888-1964

**The first woman Alberta elected to the House of Commons and the first to serve as Speaker, Cora Casselman had an impressive career in politics and world affairs.**

In 1943, she attended meetings in New York and Washington as a member of the Canadian Women's Committee on International Relations. She also served as advisor to the Canadian delegates at the meeting of the International Labour Organization in Philadelphia, 1944. In 1945 she was part of the Canadian delegation at the founding conference of the United Nations in San Francisco.

An article in the *Lethbridge Herald* described her: "A woman of education, a student of social problems, particularly those relating to the home and the family, she impressed Parliament with her earnestness and seriousness. It was no mere gesture of recognition of Canada's women that brought about her choice as a member of the delegation to the San Francisco conference."

Besides her federal duties, Cora was involved in community affairs in Edmonton and was active in a host of organizations such as the League of Nations Society, the Council of Social Agencies, and the Child Refuge Society.

44

# Marie Louise Desrosiers Charette 1888-1978.

What is it worth to have someone help deliver your baby, when you live in an isolated farm-area bereft of doctors? New mothers must have voiced their thanks for the presence of Marie Louise Desrosiers Charette, a nurse who came with her veteran husband to a Soldiers' Settlement farm at Tawatinaw, 100 miles north of Edmonton.

Marie Louise soon found herself filling all manner of medical needs. She delivered more than 400 babies during her 34 years as the only registered nurse in Tawatinaw. A young bride herself, she had graduated from Ottawa's Misericordia hospital in 1915. Life in the north was full of surprises. In 1921 a cyclone swept away newly-erected farm buildings, but the Charettes stayed with the land for 26 years, raising one son.

In the early days, Marie Louise travelled by lumber wagon and sleigh, delivering babies by the light of kerosene lamps. Setting bones and meeting other medical emergencies were also part of her life. In 1930, she organized the Red Cross chapter at Tawatinaw. In 1945, she moved with her family to Edmonton, where she lived until her death in 1978.

# Maydell Cazier Palmer (born 1889)

Teacher Maydell Cazier Palmer was active in the work of the Church of Jesus Christ of the Latter Day Saints (LDS) for more than 60 years, teaching in and leading various youth and women's organizations of the church.

Born in Utah, Maydell attended university there. She moved to Alberta in 1912 to teach English in the first high school in Raymond, the Knight Academy run by the LDS. She taught at the academy from 1912 to 1915 and again from 1918 to 1922. Maydell married Asael Palmer in 1916 and raised four children. By 1922 she was back teaching, this time in LDS auxiliary organizations. She was often on the executive of these same organizations. When her husband went to Pakistan as a director of agricultural research, Maydell taught children there.

Also active in University Women's Club, she was a charter member of the Lethbridge group and president one year. She was appointed provincial director of all the Alberta clubs and served from 1961 to 1963. Maydell was still teaching Sunday School in Lethbridge at age 87.

# Alice Mailhot Ross  1890-1968

**Alice Mailhot grew up wanting to be a civil engineer like her father. Her parents discouraged this ambition, but they allowed her to study architecture. Thus she became Canada's first woman architect.**

Educated at the Sacred Heart Convent in Calgary, Alice completed four years of study at the Rhode Island School of Design, New York, graduating in 1910. Returning to Alberta, she found there was no work for a female architect, so she went to work for the Alberta Lumber Company. Alice met her husband Hugh V. Ross, and some years later they moved to Duffield, where Hugh started his own lumber company. Occasionally Alice drew up the plans and blueprints for the business.

When her husband died in 1944, she moved her family to Edmonton and became associated with a construction firm designing a project for the National Housing Scheme. In 1948 she completed postgraduate work at the Rhode Island School of Design and returned to set up her own architectural firm, Ross Home Plans, which specialized in home designing.


# Olive Margaret Fisher   (died in 1979)

**Olive Fisher had a profound influence on the development of schools in Southern Alberta through her training of 10,000 teachers at the Calgary Normal School and the Calgary branch of the Faculty of Education. She was also the author of widely used textbooks in social studies and geography.**

Born in Bailieboro, Ontario, Olive Fisher took her early teacher training at the University of Toronto and taught for three years in the Ontario school system. In 1912, she was asked by Dr. John T. Ross to join his staff at the Calgary Normal School. She became a special instructor in primary methods, a position she held for the next 38 years. The thousands of teachers who came under the influence of her enthusiastic teaching doubtlessly taught thousands of students of their own. Some of her former pupils nominated her for an honourary doctorate, which she received from the University of Alberta in 1950, becoming the first woman educator earning that distinction.

A long-time member of the Canadian Authors' Association, Olive wrote the well-known text, *A First Geography of Canada*, and co-authored *Totem, Tipi and Tumpline*. She earned a master's degree in arts from Stanford University.

# Martha 'Mattie' Murphy Edwards   1890-1977

**A model of Alberta homesteading women, Mattie Murphy Edwards, carved a home out of the bush for her husband and 11 children in the early 1900s.**

In 1910 Mattie's father, Jordan Murphy, took his sons to northern Alberta from their home in Oklahoma to escape the segregation laws the state had enacted. Mattie's fiance, Jefferson Edwards, followed them. He soon asked Mattie to join him at Edmonton, where they were married before continuing on to a homestead in the Athabasca country.

Mattie arrived in the middle of the coldest November she had ever known. Together, she and Jeff built a home near her father's place at Pine Creek and started a family, becoming leaders of the small community later known as Amber Valley. Mattie is believed to have been the first woman in the area. They worked to have roads improved, a school built, and a church and post office established. Jeff had to take jobs off the homestead to keep it going, and Mattie did the farm chores in his absence. When her children were small, she had to tend 13 cows at a time. Mattie's long years of farming and housework left her with severe arthritis in her old age. She died in Edmonton in 1977.

# Sister Mary of the Annunciation, O.C.

**In 1969, Reverend Sister Mary of the Annunciation was made an officer of the Order of Canada, only the second woman in Alberta to be so honoured. But she would have said that her 60 years of work with less fortunate children was the only reward she needed. After all, the religious order to which she belonged pledged themselves to works of mercy for orphans and neglected children. It was their duty.**

Sister Annunciation and four other sisters arrived in Edmonton in 1912. They established their first home, The Good Shepherd, but because they had very little money, they did all their own work – milking cows, tending gardens, raising their own funds. On one occasion, Sister Annunciation and a companion traveled by hand-car into the mining towns of southern Alberta in search of funds to keep their work going. In 1927, a second, larger home was donated to the order, the O'Connell Home, and even more children were cared for.

In 1950, Sister Annunciation became Mother Superior of the Order in Edmonton and in 1962 she retired. Citations were received through the years from Popes Pius XI, Pius XII, and John XXIII and Queen Elizabeth II.

# Mabel Patrick 1891-1974

**Education was important to Mabel Patrick.**
Because there was no high school in Yorkton, Saskatchewan, Mabel travelled to school in Quebec. Then she went on to colleges in Ontario. Mabel was a gold medallist when she graduated with honours in home economics at the University of Toronto. In 1915 Mabel's career took her to the University of Manitoba where she helped to start the second Canadian degree course in household economics. Three years later, she moved on to the University of Alberta (U of A) to establish the third. The department, with Mabel as director, became a school within the Faculty of Arts and Science in 1928.

"Mabel Patrick was a good teacher. She spoke in a soft voice, and her students listened," one student remembered.

Mabel had taken time out to earn her master's degree at Columbia University. She also earned many honours during her career. She was awarded an honourary doctor of laws degree by U of A in 1965, and she received the Centennial Medal in 1967 for valuable service to the nation. The Mabel Patrick Annual Scholarship was set up by the Alberta Home Economics Association in 1945.

# Isabella Little Stevens, C.M. 1891-1980

**Isabella Little Stevens is remembered for her unstinting efforts in and for a multitude of community and social welfare organizations – 32 by one count – and for her time and work as a Calgary city alderman for seven years.**

Isabella arrived in Calgary from Quebec on the last day of the 1912 Stampede, the first ever held. Maybe that imbued her with extra energy for she proceeded to be part of the founding of Calgary's John Howard Society, the Providence Creche, the Calgary Family Service Bureau, the Catholic Family Service, the Canadian Citizenship Council, and the Council of Christians and Jews. She worked within the Catholic Women's League at all levels, the Library Board, and the Canadian Women's Press Club, to name just a few.

Somehow Isabella fit a professional career and family life into her life as well. She served for 46 years as legal editor for a firm of Calgary law publishers, and she and her husband Hermon raised a son and daughter. Isabella's amazing energy and dedication to community causes won her admittance to the Order of Canada in 1976 and an honourary degree from the University of Calgary in 1965.

# Sister Agnes Carroll

**Little is known about Sister Agnes Carroll personally, but her reputation in establishing Holy Cross Hospital in Calgary lives on.** Sister Agnes Carroll arrived from Montreal as the Superior of three other Grey Nuns, in January, 1891; she remained the dedicated Superior of the Sisters of Charity there until 1907.

Sister Agnes Carroll, with Sisters Beauchemin, Valiquette, and Gertrude arrived with only $73.75 to establish a hospital in a 24-square foot building. The first floor was for patients, the second for the Sisters. The hospital quickly outgrew the facilities, and Sister Agnes Carroll set about raising funds for a larger building. Two of the Sisters even travelled the Calgary/Edmonton railway seeking donations from workers. Less than two years later, the new 50-foot-square, three-storey building opened. During the 1892 smallpox epidemic, the Sisters staffed a tent hospital a few miles outside of town; by the 1893 diphtheria epidemic they were able to use the unfinished third floor of the hospital as an isolation ward.

By the time Sister Agnes Carroll left in 1907, Holy Cross Hospital was well established and had obtained its certificate as a nursing school.

# Elizabeth Patteson Tayler  (born 1891)

**Elizabeth Patteson Tayler was named a 1945 Edmonton citizen of the year for her work with hospitalized soldiers and the blind. The award summed up a lifetime of service to her community.**

Bessie Tayler was born at Fort Macleod where her father was with the North West Mounted Police. She trained as a nurse at Galt Hospital, Lethbridge and was one of three in the hospital's first graduating class. She married Arnold Tayler, just before he went overseas in 1916. She soon followed, joining the British Red Cross Auxiliary – the Canadian Army did not accept married nurses – and was in charge of a Berkshire Auxiliary hospital.

The Taylers next moved to Edmonton, and Bessie began a 50-year career in community service. She worked tirelessly for the Victorian Order of Nurses, Women's Canadian Club, Imperial Order of Daughters of the Empire, and other groups. When World War II started, she went back to the Red Cross and was on the executives of Air Force Mothers, the War Service Council, and the United Services Association, providing entertainment and hospital visits for soldiers. After the war, she  spearheaded the Emily Murphy Pavilion project, and worked to have Roberta MacAdams' portrait hung in the Legislature.

# Georgina 'Georgie' Helen Thomson 1892-1963

**Innovative librarian Georgina 'Georgie' Helen Thomson did more than love the books in her care. She added to their number by writing her own.**

Georgina was born into a Galt, Ontario family that had originally emigrated from Scotland. Her father, George Thomson, joined neighbours who moved to the Parkland district in Alberta in 1904. For two years, Georgina and her four sisters and brother were educated at home by their mother, a graduate of Toronto Normal. When Sleepy Hollow public school was built, they attended it. Georgie's account of homesteading days and her school experiences were in her book, *Crocus and Meadowlark Country*.

Georgie went to Normal School herself and taught. She followed up with a 1919 arts degree from the University of Alberta, winning two gold medals. A few more years of teaching led her to the Calgary library, where she proved to be an innovative librarian for 34 years. Georgie also studied extramurally to obtain a master's degree in 1925, and contributed both prose and poetry using the pseudonyms 'Pyrrha' and 'Heather MacPhail.' A book reviewer called her one "whose name became synonymous with arts and letters in Alberta."

# Jessie Louise Purves Church 1892-1972

**Jessie Church was clear in her intentions. If children needed health services or education or welfare, she would organize a group to help. That's why she brought the Junior Red Cross and the Girl Guides to Alberta, and that's why she organized a Muscular Dystrophy Association. Whatever worked with and for young people.**

Trained in social work at McGill, Jessie came to Calgary in 1919 as welfare officer for the federal Department of Pensions. The job involved travel all over Alberta and British Columbia to determine the needs of children of service men killed or injured in World War I. This led to Jessie's efforts to give children training and support in life skills. That's when she took a leave of absence from her job to organize Alberta branches of the Junior Red Cross, a club for young people whose motto matched her own: health, service, and international understanding. Jessie stayed with Red Cross as a volunteer for the next 50 years.

The Girl Guide movement had not yet moved into Alberta. Jessie got it going and for years spent her vacations taking young Guides to camp. Ditto with the Muscular Dystrophy Association.

# Mary Barter Cody  1892-1975

**Mary Barter Cody survived the dreaded Spanish flu in 1918, thanks in part to the care she received at the small hospital in Cereal, Alberta.  As a result, she stayed on at the hospital to help other flu patients and ended up nursing there for the next 30 years, 17 of those years as matron.**

During the Depression in the 1930s, nurse Cody and Dr. Esler were a good team: he travelled all over the area, she stayed at the hospital and managed to be both nurse and everything else – cook, midwife, housekeeper, accountant, laundress.  On call 24 hours a day, she kept up an incredible schedule that required both stamina and imagination.  For instance, when ether was used as an anaesthetic, all fires had to be extinguished or there was the risk of explosion.  That meant that the babies had to be moved into the kitchen, the warmest place in the hospital, and lights had to be rigged up from a car battery.

In the 1940s, the hospital was taken over by the municipality and running water was finally installed.  The community showed its gratitude with a Mary Cody Day in 1968, and she in turn showed her gratitude by saying, "I've had my roses while living."

# Cornelia Railey Wood  1892-1985

**Six terms set the record.  When Cornelia Railey Wood completed her sixth term in 1967 as a member of the Alberta Legislative Assembly, she had achieved a Canadian record for women members of a legislative assembly (MLAs).  Cornelia was Social Credit MLA for Stony Plain for 1940 to 1955 and from 1959 to 1967, a total of 23 years.**

Like so many women in the early days, Cornelia began her working life as a school teacher.  After marriage to Russell Wood of Stony Plain, she continued her community involvement as a member and officer of the local, provincial, and national Women's Institutes.  From there, she moved on to become chairman of the Stony Plain Consolidated School Board, chairman of the Alberta division of the Community Planning Association of Canada, and MLA for Stony Plain.  Somewhere in there, she was also mayor of Stony Plain.

In 1981, Cornelia was named a 'Persons Award' winner.  There are five of these awards given each year by the Governor-General to selected Canadian women.  And in 1982, Stony Plain named her Citizen of the Year.

# Agnes Aston Hill  1893-1964

**Maybe it was the move to a new Calgary home, Tanglewood, that induced Agnes Aston Hill to write poetry beginning in the 1930s.**

Agnes, born and raised in England, came to Canada to marry Henry Hill. They had two children and moved to Calgary in 1914. She began to write poetry for publication not long after the family moved into Tanglewood, their second Calgary home. Her poetry, articles, and stories appeared in many publications, both in North America and in England. In 1941, Agnes won first prize in a nationwide contest, a silver medal from the governor-general for one of her war poems. Two years before she died a collection of her poetry was published.

Agnes also became a *Calgary Herald* columnist, 'Aunt Marian.' She wrote *Junior's Corner* on the care of animals for young people. She wrote the column for a decade, from 1930 to 1940. Agnes was a member and strong supporter of the Society for the Prevention of Cruelty to Animals; she was also a member of the Canadian Authors Association. She was especially fond of England, although she never returned home after emigrating.

# Hazel Rutherford McCuaig  1893-1992

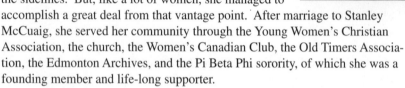

**Hazel Rutherford watched from the sidelines during the official celebrations in Edmonton  that made Alberta a new province in 1905 and made her father Alexander Rutherford the first premier.  Four years later, she watched from the sidelines as her father plowed the first furrows to prepare land for the first university in the province, the University of Alberta. And when her parents built a large house near the university, she watched that happening too.**

In fact, Hazel Rutherford seemed always to be on the sidelines. But, like a lot of women, she managed to accomplish a great deal from that vantage point. After marriage to Stanley McCuaig, she served her community through the Young Women's Christian Association, the church, the Women's Canadian Club, the Old Timers Association, the Edmonton Archives, and the Pi Beta Phi sorority, of which she was a founding member and life-long supporter.

When her father died, Hazel donated her share of his extensive Canadiana collection of books to the university library, and the university recognized this contribution and others with an honourary degree in 1964. In the 1970s, the family home was restored as Rutherford House.

# Florence E.C. Reid  1894-1981

**Florence Reid did everything she could to provide a homelike atmosphere for patients as director of nursing at the Junior Red Cross Crippled Children's Hospital in Calgary for almost 20 years.**

After nurses' training, Florence started out as a public health nurse, teaching at Vermilion Agricultural College during the school year and working as a public health nurse in the summers. She worked as a district health nurse out of Hanna and then in the Peace River area. She joined the Alberta division of the Canadian Red Cross Society in 1932, and her long career at the children's hospital started the next year.

While director of nursing, Florence started both the hospital's outpatient department and the brace shop. Most of all though she worked vigorously to keep the hospital from being an 'institution' to its patients, many of whom were in for long-term care. Social activities were arranged and Scout, Cub, Guide, and Brownie groups were organized. In 1952, Florence became the hospital's director of public relations, staying in that job until her 1961 retirement. In 1954, she was named a Calgary Citizen of the Year for her work at the children's hospital.

# Edith Cox Rogers  1894-1985

**In 1929, the stock market crashed, and William and Edith Rogers moved to Calgary. Those two facts came together when the Rogers met their new neighbour, William Aberhart, a proponent of a new political party called Social Credit. Its economic policies held the solution, he suggested, to the worldwide depression. The Rogers agreed with him so enthusiastically that Edith agreed to run in Ponoka as a candidate in 1935, the first time Social Credit ever appeared on the ballot in Alberta. It was a sweep: Social Credit, and Edith Rogers found themselves in the Alberta legislature.**

During an afternoon session of the legislature, Edith was asked to serve as the Speaker of the Assembly. It was a temporary arrangement, but it was a first for a woman, nevertheless, to preside as Speaker of a provincial legislature.

In 1940, the family moved to Edmonton where Edith continued her public life as public school board trustee for 15 years. In private life, she collected stories of Edmonton pioneers and published them in a book, *History Made in Edmonton*. When the Edith Rogers Junior High School was opened in 1975, Edith began giving a copy of her book to every grade 9 graduate.

53

# Catharine 'Katie' McCrimmon Love  1895-1930

**Although her life was brief, Catherine 'Katie' McCrimmon Love packed a great deal into it. She was the first woman president of a student body, she taught school, she was provincial Girls' Work Secretary with the Young Women's Christian Association (YWCA), she married and had three daughters.**

Katie moved to Edmonton, where she graduated from the University of Alberta in 1917. At university, she was active on the YWCA, the Literary Society, the Athletic Society, and the Wauneita Society. She was the first woman elected president of a Students' Union, in 1916. In 1929, she became the first woman member of the university senate. After working as the Edmonton YWCA, Katie studied at Edmonton Normal, later teaching at Queen's Avenue school. Social service attracted her back, however, and she became provincial YMCA Girls' Work Secretary.

When in 1925 she married J. R. Love, hundreds of young girls in uniform serenaded her with the campfire song, *Marinka, We Love You.* The mother of three small girls, Katie was expecting to leave hospital in 1930 when she suddenly died, evoking sorrow across the province and expressions of gratitude for her life of service.

# Catherine Brodie Andrews  1895-1967

**Catherine Brodie pinned her long red hair into a bun and started teaching school at 16 years of age. From then on, she never changed her hair style and never changed her dedication to education.**

After 10 years of teaching in southern Alberta, Kate married William Andrews, had three daughters, and put the shoe on the other foot. She became a school trustee, first for 13 years on the local White School Board and then for 24 years on the board of the Lethbridge School Division. Women were still fairly rare birds in public life; Catherine was the first woman on the Lethbridge School Board and when she became chairman of the board, she was the first woman to serve as such.

The Lethbridge Junior College (now Lethbridge Community College) came into existence in 1956, thanks largely to Catherine, who had done detailed research on community-based colleges. It was another first in Canada. She served as chairman of the college board from 1957 to 1967; she also served on the Senate of the University of Alberta and was granted an honourary degree from them in 1966. Two buildings were named for the lady with the bun, one at the Lethbridge Community College and a high school in Coaldale.

# Iva Pearl Marshall McLeod 1895-1975

**Iva Marshall's arrival in Cold Lake in June 1921 was an adventure, one of the many she would have there.**

Iva was a 1919 graduate of the Misericordia Hospital, Edmonton. To get to Cold Lake, where she went as medical personnel for the Presbyterian Missionary Society, she travelled by train to St. Paul, to Bonnyville by mail truck (an old, topless touring car), and finally by team and democrat. Iva lived in a room over a store. Her office was a log building formerly used to store fish. She converted the office to a hospital when her first patient, a man with pneumonia, rode into town. The community supplied bed and bedding, the fishermen supplied ice to reduce the man's fever. Water was carried in buckets from the lake until a pulley was installed. This was the beginning of the John Neill hospital, which officially opened in 1926.

Iva rode a horse on her district nursing trips. That was no small feat since the horse liked to pitch off riders by sudden jumps sideways. In 1922 Iva left Cold Lake to marry Fred McLeod. However, she returned after two years and continued helping the nursing staff at night. At Cold Lake, Chapter 46 of the Alberta Association of Registered Nurses is named for her.

# Gladys McKelvie Egbert 1896-1968

**At the age of 12, Gladys Egbert became the youngest person ever to receive a three-year scholarship from the Royal Academy of Music, London, England.**

She later studied at the Juilliard School of Music in New York, where she was offered an important piano teaching position. Instead she chose to return to Calgary in 1920 to begin teaching. Her students, many of whom came great distances for weekly lessons, won numerous national and international awards. Gladys herself returned at intervals to New York, to continue her music study. Her 48-year career as an outstanding music teacher ended only at her death in 1968. Her colleagues honoured her by establishing the Memorial Rose Bowl, presented each year to the most outstanding performer at the Alberta Music Festival.

Gladys married William Gordon Egbert in 1924, and they raised one son and one daughter. Gladys received an honourary doctorate of laws from the University of Alberta at Calgary in 1965, and the 1967 Centennial Award from the Canadian Music Teachers' Federation.

# Lily Lee Kwong 1896-1975

**Lily Lee Kwong was a trailblazer, assuming responsibility for the welfare of Calgary's growing Chinese community and raising funds for various causes.**

Lily was born in China and joined her parents in Victoria, British Columbia in 1912 when she was 16. She worked in their store, helped with housework, and took care of her siblings. She married Charlie Kwong and moved to Calgary, raising a family of six. Her trailblazing began after the children grew up, when she cast aside her traditional role to become a community activist. It started in the late 1930s when she became concerned about refugees from the Sino-Japanese War. Lily raised funds, rallying local Chinese women to the cause and sending a considerable sum of money to China for relief efforts.

Local issues next drew her attention, especially the plight of the Chinese United Church, which was under-funded in its efforts to provide social services among the Chinese. After founding the Mother's Club at the church, Lily hit upon an interesting fund-raiser: chow mein teas. These evolved into mammoth, twice-annual affairs, drawing 1500 people at a time. Lily is credited with setting a precedent for other women to follow.

# Betty Mitchell 1896-1976

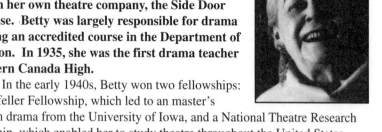

**Betty Mitchell was Calgary's first lady of theatre for more than 30 years. Her interest in drama began in her university days when she acted and directed plays. In 1924 she founded the Green Room Club and then her own theatre company, the Side Door Playhouse. Betty was largely responsible for drama becoming an accredited course in the Department of Education. In 1935, she was the first drama teacher at Western Canada High.**

In the early 1940s, Betty won two fellowships: a Rockefeller Fellowship, which led to an master's degree in drama from the University of Iowa, and a National Theatre Research Fellowship, which enabled her to study theatre throughout the United States. Returning to Calgary in 1944, she founded Workshop 14, a theatre study group for graduate students which turned out more than 100 professional actors and theatrical workers.

In 1968, Workshop 14 was renamed Theatre Calgary and became a fully professional group. In 1980, four years after her death, Theatre Calgary announced the formation of a $25,000 trust fund in Betty's honour to develop and train young theatre professionals.

# Martha Isabel Houston  (born 1896)

**Art was High River high school teacher Martha Houston's special interest, and she managed to include it in her teaching whenever she could.**

Martha was born in Newark, New Jersey, and came to Alberta as a teenager. After schooling in Denver, Colorado, and in Calgary, she attended the University of Denver, graduating with a bachelor's degree in 1918. For the next 11 years, she kept house for her father. In 1930, she resumed her schooling, taking teacher's training in Calgary. She taught 11 years at Magrath and 13 at High River, where she settled after her retirement.

Her interest in art went back many years. Whenever she could, she taught art classes in the high schools where she worked. Martha attended the Banff School of Fine Arts for many summers. She joined the Calgary Artist Society and, when the Calgary Allied Art Centre opened, became a member of it. Martha was deeply involved in the effort to bring stimulating art to smaller centres of population, and organized the High River Art Club in 1947, hoping to increase the interest of local people in art.

# Marie Anna Roy  (born 1896)

**Marie Anna Roy was a teacher first, a homesteader second, and then a writer.**

Born in a French Manitoba town, St. Leon, Marie Anna spent her childhood there and in St. Boniface. She went to Normal School, first in Winnipeg and then in Edmonton. She also studied at Queen's University and the University of Alberta. She was a bilingual teacher and taught at Tangent for a number of years, facing isolation and hardship for a low salary. After a severe accident, she left teaching and began homesteading near Tangent. She lived alone, breaking the sod and tilling the land herself.

Marie Anna began her most successful career, as a writer, working at nights on her homestead. She published eight books in all. Marie Anna wrote a history of the French in Manitoba as well as fictional stories based on her family. Her manuscripts are archived in Quebec, Manitoba, and Alberta. Much of her writing is based on the pioneer parishes of northern Alberta. She is one of 35 French Canadian women honoured in a photo album commemorating the 60th anniversary of La Federation des Femmes Canadiennes-Francais.

# Fern Wood Smith  (born 1896)

**What's a woman to do when her husband dies leaving her with three children aged six, four, and two? Move into town and start making chocolates, that's what.**

Fern and Frank Wood farmed at Hill Spring, 20 miles from Cardston. They had a new house, three healthy children, good land, but along came the flu. Frank lived through it but died shortly after from a heart attack. Fern decided to rent the farm and live off the rent, but the Dirty Thirties arrived. The farm didn't produce enough income to support the young family, so Fern took in boarders, baked and decorated wedding cakes, and made bread for customers. Then one day, she remembered the chocolates that she'd seen in production in Salt Lake City when she went to school there. Maybe chocolates would sell?

They would. Eventually, Fern's Chocolates became well known in the area, and Fern bought herself an electric beater for the enormous sum of $750. It was the best investment she could have made. She made enough money to build her own house with a special area set aside in the basement for a small efficient chocolate factory.

## Minnie McLean Villett

**In 1969, Minnie McLean Villett was the first woman ever to receive an honourary doctorate of divinity degree from St. Stephen's College in Edmonton. In fact, she was only the second lay person to ever receive the honour previously reserved for clergy only.**

The degree was given in recognition of her 45 years of active service and leadership at all levels in the United Church of Canada, but she explained modestly that it was "an honour to the work of all women in the Church rather than a personal award." When she married Rev. G. Harrison Villett in 1923, Minnie entered into his ministry with all the training and energy she had. In Iron Springs, Taber, Pincher Creek, Edmonton, and Vancouver, she taught Sunday School and Bible study groups, led youth groups, participated in women's church groups, participated in community groups such as Women's Christian Temperance Union and Local Council of Women, taught at Alberta College, and represented Alberta and British Columbia at General Council of the United Church of Canada.

The idealism and dedication demonstrated at a student volunteer meeting she attended influenced her for the rest of her life.

# Maud 'Peggy' Lewis Holmes  (born 1897)

**In a life filled with 'firsts,' Peggy Holmes was, at 16, the first woman to work in a bank in the north of England.**

Coming to Canada in 1919 as a war bride, she went with her husband Harry to homestead in the Ashmont area, moving later to Edmonton. The mother of four children, Peggy had only one son survive; her three daughters died at birth. She became a music teacher and community worker, helping found the Edmonton branch of the Cancer Society. Her volunteer service also included board member for the Young Women's Christian Association, Victorian Order of Nurses, the Red Cross, and as secretary for Women's Volunteer Services during World War II.

At 60, Peggy turned to painting, exhibiting widely and selling successfully. Finally, at 77, she took a creative writing course at a senior citizens' centre. She sent a few scripts to Canadian Broadcasting Corporation radio, and soon had her own program, *The Way It Was*. In a three-year period, she produced 460 scripts  She later described them as "off the cuff and the top of my head . . . a mixed bag!"  In 1977, Peggy received the Alberta Achievement Award for Excellence.

# Dellamen Plamondon Chévigny Proulx  (born 1897)

**Daughter of the pioneer after whom the village of Plamondon was named, Dellamen Plamondon arrived in Alberta in 1908, aged 11, and became the only white child at the Lac la Biche Mission School. At the age of 12, she took charge of a school in the Plamondon settlement and began her life-long career of unpaid community service.**

As the first organist of the Church of Saint Isidore, she became the musical leader of the community, organizing concerts and directing plays. She assisted her father in providing health care to the area and showed heroism in her nursing of the sick during the influenza epidemic of 1919/1920. From 1920 to 1935, she was the local midwife. The mother of six children, she also raised many orphans and cared for an indigent elderly citizen.

Married in 1911 to Albert Chévigny, she helped him open the first general store and the first hotel in Plamondon. After the death of her first husband, she married Octave Chévigny in 1935. Widowed again in 1962, she married her third husband, René Proulx, in 1966. On her 77th birthday in 1974, the people of Plamondon  honoured Dellamen Plamondon Chévigny Proulx for her lifelong generosity toward those in need.

# Antoinette Babin Biron  1897-1973

Antoinette Biron's life, like most pioneers' lives, was one of hard work and dedication to her family. Most of all she wanted a church in her community, feeling that without one the social environment was not complete. When the Beaver Mines Roman Catholic Church opened in 1934, funded and built by towns-people, it was a gratifying accomplishment for every member of the community, especially Antoinette.

Arriving from her native Austria in 1913, Antoinette joined her parents on their ranch. She married Guillaume Biron, another pioneer rancher, two years later. They raised a family of 10 daughters and one son. Antoinette spun her own wool and made all the family clothing by hand. She was also concerned with outside influences on her children, and was determined that they get the best education possible. Her contributions ranged from helping with Christmas concerts to serving as school trustee.

Her persuasive arguments finally resulted in her community financing and building St. Anthony of Padua Church. The fund-raising activities included dances, pie socials, turkey shoots, and raffles. Besides participating energetically in these, Antoinette prepared many meals for those building the church.

# Elizabeth 'Lizzie' Rummel  1897-1980

Elizabeth Lizzie Rummel was one of Banff's more colourful old-timers, a breezy, informal woman whose trademark was the eternal 'roll-your-own' dangling from a corner of her mouth. She was an endless source of anecdotes and information on the Rockies.

Born to a titled Bavarian family, Lizzie grew up in a 22-room house with servants and a butler. In 1911, her mother decided the family would benefit from the rugged life and purchased an Alberta ranch as a summer home. Without passage to Germany and without funds in 1914, the Rummel women ran the ranch themselves. Lizzie adapted easily, becoming adept at handling a horse and acquiring considerable managerial skills.

In 1936, she left the ranch for Banff, where she began the guiding that was to occupy her for the next 30 years. In 1949, she bought her own lodge near Mount Assiniboine and ran a small but successful operation, providing warm hospitality and expert guidance in skiing, riding, and hiking. Her guests from around the world were convinced that in Lizzie's vibrant presence they experienced a deeper appreciation of the beauty and wonder of the Rockies.

# Elizabeth Sterling Haynes  1898-1957

**One fine day in 1933, Elizabeth Sterling Haynes said, "Let's start a school of drama at Banff." It was the middle of the Depression, drama wasn't exactly a priority in Alberta right then, but lo and behold, 200 students turned up, and a school was born. The school had drama as one of its most important elements, and it was named the Banff School of Fine Arts.**

Elizabeth Sterling Haynes trained and worked as an actress in Toronto and New York before moving to Edmonton with her husband in the early 1920s. It wasn't long before Edmonton realized a revolution was brewing in their theatre world. Elizabeth founded the University of Alberta's Studio Theatre, the Alberta Drama League, and the Canadian Women's Theatre Guild. Then she took on the province, travelling everywhere on behalf of the government to encourage local theatre. In between her official duties, she acted in, directed, produced, and adjudicated plays.

When she received the 1944 Citizen of the Year award in Edmonton, Elizabeth was described as a "valiant servant of the theatre."

# Aileen Hackett Fish, C.M.  1898-1977

**Appointed a member of the Order of Canada in 1973 for her outstanding community service for more than 30 years, Aileen Hackett Fish was one of Calgary's most active women in civic and community affairs.**

With a degree in honours English and history from McGill University, Aileen taught school in Lloydminster and Calgary before marrying Dr. Frank Fish in 1921. As their three children grew up, she took on more and more volunteer activities outside the home: Home and School, the Young Women's Christian Association, the City of Calgary Development Appeal Board, the Advisory Board of the National Library of Canada, the Council of Women, Beta Sigma Phi, the Women's Canadian Club, and the Women's Conservative Association.

Aileen also taught business deportment for a local business school, taught English for New Canadians through the Calgary School Board, and served as advisor to women students at the University of Calgary (U of C). A popular speaker, she often delivered humor and history to audiences. In 1976, she received an honourary degree from the U of C.

# Hanka Romanchych Kowalchuk 1898-1984

**Hanka Kowalchuk observed that prairie men had continuous contact with each other, meeting in "beer parlours, implement stores, elevators. But women? Almost never." She made it her vocation to change that fact.**

Hanka grew up in a community-minded, politically active Dauphin, Manitoba family. In 1926 she was a founding member of the Ukrainian Women's Association of Canada. In 1928 she came to Alberta as a district worker for the Women's Bureau, coordinating all community work except health. She led 326 groups of women representing a multitude of ethnic origins. The women were hesitant to step into community life. Hanka worked hard and imaginatively to get them out of their homes and actively involved.

During the 1930s, she organized groups to help women supplement family income by producing and selling embroidery, weaving, and painted Easter eggs. This led to her lasting interest in Ukrainian handicrafts. Her concern for the status and welfare of women everywhere led to her participation in a 1936 panel on the status of women for the League of Nations. During World War II she was active in the National Council of Women.

# Imelda Pépin Olsen 1899-1975

**The musical talent of five-year-old Imelda Pépin shone as she accompanied her kindergarten class in a Dawson City concert. That talent was to shine for years to come, both as a performer and as a composer.**

Born at St. Lambert, Quebec, Imelda began her musical career in the Yukon after her family moved there. But she was sent to Quebec for schooling and musical training. Returning west, to Edmonton, Imelda studied for many years under both Madame Le Saunier and Hugh Bancroft, an organist. She earned LRSM and ATCM special diplomas. At age fifteen, she was assistant organist at the Immaculate Conception Church. When the church was replace by St. Joseph's Cathedral, Imelda became the organist there too.

As well as being an outstanding teacher, Imelda was a composer. Two of her pieces, *Mass in Honour of St. Joseph* and *Regina Ceoli*, were performed at the cathedral. Imelda married and had five children. Her passion for music led her to be choral director for the Edmonton Civic Opera and official accompanist for the Edmonton Catholic Schools at music festivals and massed choir demonstrations.

# Annora Brown 1899-1987

**Born and raised in Fort Macleod, Annora Brown painted what she could see around her – prairie flowers, grain elevators, sun-baked grassy hillsides, old buildings, and native people.**

Sometimes she put them all together as she did in her book called *Old Man's Garden*, in which she recorded and illustrated native legends relating to the flowers and plants of southern Alberta. It's a rare and valuable book now, but it wasn't when she first did it. She had to teach school and give art lessons to support her painting habit until one of her paintings, *Prairie Chicken Dance*, was selected in 1955 to form the basis of a provincial art collection. That established Annora as a serious artist, and she began to get larger commissions. Glenbow Foundation, for example, asked for 200 watercolors of Alberta wild flowers.

Annora also enjoyed handicrafts and designed some 100 formalized motifs of western themes, birds, fences, the seasons, for reproduction in needlework and hooked rugs. She was the only woman founding member of the Alberta Society of Artists, and she was the first woman to receive an honourary degree from the University of Lethbridge.

# Susan 'Susie' Wright Atkinson 1899-1991

**'Bloom where you're planted' must have been Susie Wright Atkinson's motto.**

She was only 16 when her mother died, which meant she had to stay home to look after her four younger brothers and sisters. Later, when her husband Edward Atkinson, a St. Albert area farmer, died, she had to look after their farm as well as three young children. Somehow, she found time to be active in the local Women's Institute, to lead a 4H club, and to work for a library and church for the town of St. Albert.

In 1956, she and her son moved to a Lacombe area farm where they raised purebred cattle, several times prize winners at the Royal Winter Fair in Toronto. It was then that Susie was elected councillor for the county of Lacombe, the first woman in Alberta to be named a county councillor. She also became the first woman to be admitted to the Hall of Fame at Olds Agricultural and Vocational College.

Once retired from farming, Susie turned her attention to the needs of seniors, serving on the Board of the Lacombe Nursing Home while it was being built, serving as president of the Lacombe Friendship Club, and helping to establish the Kosy Korner, a drop-in centre.

# Rae McIntyre Chittick, C.M. 1899-1992

**Rae Chittick devoted her life to public health education in Canada and internationally.**

Born in Ontario, but raised and educated in Calgary, Rae attended normal school before studying nursing at Johns Hopkins Hospital in Baltimore. She later went on to obtain three other degrees: bachelor of nursing, Teachers College, Columbia University; master's of arts in education, Stanford University; and a master's in public health, Harvard University.

After nursing school, Rae went into public health nursing with the Victorian Order of Nurses in British Columbia and then the Saskatchewan Department of Public Health. In 1926 she started her public health education career with the Provincial Normal School, Calgary. When the school became a part of the University of Alberta in 1945, she had the rank of assistant and then associate professor. In 1953, she began a 10-year appointment as director, School for Graduate Nurses, McGill University. On her retirement, Rae moved into international public health education, working with the World Health Organization in Ghana, Jamaica, Guatemala, and Australia. She was named to the Order of Canada in 1975.

# Rose Pearson Kohn 1900-1967

**In 1968 the Rose Kohn Memorial Arena was opened in Calgary in tribute to a community volunteer who had worked unceasingly for 25 years to improve sporting opportunities for city youth.**

It started in 1926 when Rose and Herman Kohn emigrated to Alberta, living in Edmonton and on a farm near Millet before moving to Calgary around 1940. The mother of five sons, Rose devoted time and energy to community activities. Believing sports fostered good citizenship, she worked to provide interesting and wholesome recreation for youngsters. Rose organized baseball and basketball leagues, promoted community figure skating, and was a vocal supporter of sports for girls. But hockey was her main interest, particularly minor hockey. She started in the 1940s with eight clubs and approximately 300 boys; by 1967 the numbers totalled 240 teams and 3,800 boys.

The work that the hockey league entailed was phenomenal, but Rose was the person to do it. Rose contacted organizations, handled finances, prepared schedules, coordinated leagues, arranged for referees, and helped with events such as Minor Hockey Night in Canada and annual tournaments.

# Lady Rodney (Marjorie Lowther) (died in 1968)

**Nursery care for babies in Edmonton for only 10 cents a day was one of many vital community services Lady Rodney, or Marjorie Lowther, to use her maiden name, helped organize.**

A member of the Local Council of Women, Marjorie was interested in social problems concerning children and young people. The first president of the Edmonton Creche, she was Alberta's first provincial commissioner of Girl Guides. She was well-known in Edmonton for her community involvement. She raised a family of five children, the oldest of whom was killed in battle in World War II. As a result, Marjorie welcomed countless fliers into her home, along with English children evacuated to Canada.

Marjorie and her husband Lord George Rodney came to Alberta in 1919. They bought 1,000 acres near Fort Saskatchewan and personally turned it into a successful farm. They also actively promoted British emigration to Canada. After several years raising livestock and field crops, the Rodneys decided to concentrate on breeding pigs and won many awards exhibiting their prize hogs across Canada. Active in promoting formal organization of the Girl Guides, Marjorie was an accomplished speaker who travelled widely.

# Mary 'Molly' Coupland

**The only girl in a family with eight sons, Molly Coupland learned early about lending a helping hand. And help she did, working in 35 volunteer positions over a 50-year period.**

The Couplands came to Bow Island from Scotland in 1910, when Molly's father was appointed manager of the Southern Alberta Land Company. Later Molly recalled the joy of the good old days: "We created our own entertainment – programs, pie-and-box socials. We staged dances to the music of an old gramophone in Jack Ovard's barn in 40 below zero weather, and raised enough from admission for a piano down-payment to replace the old school organ."

The power of giving, so early instilled, stayed with Molly all her life. She served in numerous volunteer positions, mostly in the McNally and Lethbridge areas, many of them connected with farm organizations or the care of the ill and elderly. In a fitting tribute, 300 friends gathered in 1971 to participate in Molly Coupland Appreciation Night, culminating in the presentation of a suitcase filled with dollar bills for Molly's trip to an Associated Country Women of the World conference in Oslo, Norway.

# Beatrice Van Loon Carmichael   (died in 1964)

**Born into a musical family of five daughters, Beatrice Van Loon sang publicly from the age of four. At 16, she conducted her first operetta, with 100 young people in the company and 50 in the orchestra.**

Her plans to go to Germany to study voice were cancelled when World War I broke out, but Beatrice's appearance singing with the Chicago Symphony led to other opportunities. She became first the conductor of first one all-girls' orchestra and then of another. When the second played for eight weeks at Edmonton's Macdonald hotel, Beatrice stayed, marrying dentist James B. Carmichael in 1920. Her musical talents were fully employed in Edmonton as she: organized the Edmonton Civic Opera Society, acted as its musical director for 28 years, played first violin in the Edmonton Symphony for 13 seasons, and conducted the forerunner of the University Philharmonic.

Beatrice also organized and conducted the CKUA Radio Orchestra and helped young musicians get started. She started an orchestra at Strathcona High School for example, and was known as 'Auntie Van' to generations of musicians and associates. Many honours were awarded to Beatrice, along with the love of countless beneficiaries of her varied musical gifts.

# Bérangère Mercier

**As a painter, vocalist, pioneer radio broadcaster, and founder of arts organizations, Bérangère Mercier made a notable contribution to Alberta's cultural development.**

Born into one of the original families of New France at St. Julie de Laurierville, Quebec, Bérangère arrived in Alberta in 1910 and settled in Edmonton in 1913. A self-taught painter of landscapes and portraits in oils, she joined the Edmonton Art Club in 1921, later serving on its executive during 45 years of membership. Murals by Bérangère became well-known features of the Marian Centre and the Catholic Information Centre.

A gifted soprano, Bérangère sang on radio CNRE in 1922, on the opening broadcast of CKUA in 1928, and on her own French-language program with CKUA from 1931 to 1933. She was a charter member of the Edmonton Civic Opera. An energetic supporter of francophone culture, she organized French concerts throughout Alberta, worked for the French program at the Banff Centre, was a long-time member of Les Bonnes Amies Club, and served as a bilingual secretary at the Edmonton Postal Service from 1935 to 1954.

# Eleanor Mountifield Vogelsong

**As captain, Eleanor Mountifield led the Edmonton Grads Basketball Team to victory in the first Canadian basketball national championship. The 1922 tournament pitted the Grads against the top eastern team, the London Shamrocks, and marked the start of their dominance on national and international levels.**

Eleanor attended McDougall Commercial High School where a young teacher named J. Percy Page introduced the new sport of basketball to female students in his physical training classes in 1914. In 1915, girls graduating from the school asked Mr. Page to coach a 'grads' team. The members devoted themselves to precision drills, swept the provincial competitions, and reigned as national champions from 1922 onward. They demonstrated their game at four Olympics, beating all European challengers, and won the North American basketball championship every year from 1934 to 1940. The Grads disbanded in 1940, having won 502 of their 522 matches.

During the dark days of the Depression, the team was a focus of Alberta pride, and the 52 women who became Grads during the team's 25-year history were famous role models for working women.

# Margaret Strang Savage  1901-1970

**When Margaret Strang graduated in medicine from the University of Western Ontario in 1929, she was the only woman in a class of 25. Two years later she was appointed by the Presbyterian Church as a medical missionary in Peace River Country.**

When the people of her district built her a combination doctor's office and manse, she pitched in too, impressing everyone by the flakiness of the pies she baked for the workers and her agility with an axe. Travelling about her large territory on horseback in all conditions, Margaret earned the respect and devotion of the people she served.

In 1933 she married Douglas Savage. Their years of homesteading and various business ventures were difficult, but Margaret saw a special virtue in them. "I've entered by another door – their door – into the lives of my Peace River people. All that we've experienced is the fabric of their life too. I'm one of them now." In 1943 she went with her family to Cold Lake, a remote village of 400 people, to be doctor of the small United Church hospital there. She soon became public health officer, and, in the 1950s, she had the satisfaction of seeing a local, modern, fully equipped hospital open.

## Irene Makuch Pawlikowski 1901-1975

**Irene Pawlikowski brought an intense interest in international women's organizations with her to Canada when she emigrated from the western Ukraine in the early 1950s. She also brought a deep love of Ukrainian arts and culture.**

Born and raised in Lviv, Irene studied law, music, and social work. She married Julian Pawlikowski, an economist and lawyer, in 1926. They had one daughter. Julian died in 1949, and Irene came to Canada. She moved to Fort Saskatchewan where her daughter lived in 1954. As one of the founding members of the World Federation of Ukrainian Women's Organizations,

Irene immediately joined the Ukrainian Catholic Women's League (UCWL). She was elected to the executive in Western Canada in 1955, serving until her death in 1975. She was president of the National UCWL of Canada, with a membership of 10,000, from 1964 to 1968.

Irene was also active with the International Alliance of Women, Mouvement Mondial des Meres, and the World Union of Catholic Women's Organizations. Her knowledge of Ukrainian handicrafts helped mold the UCWL Museum's collection in Edmonton.

# Gertrude Barrett O'Keefe, C.M. 1901-1978

**A life of service, culminating in tributes from Alberta's Lieutenant-Governor, the mayor of Calgary, the Chamber of Commerce, the Lion's Club and civic groups make up Gertrude Barrett O'Keefe's record.**

Graduating as a registered nurse from Calgary General Hospital in 1924, she married T. L. O'Keefe in 1927, had one son, and became an active worker in church and school projects. Her extensive work for the Red Cross began in 1940, along with civil defence duties and service on the Calgary Hospital Board. She served as board chairman. Gertrude's outstanding contribution was as a volunteer organizer and supervisor of the blood donor procurement program for the Red Cross, at a time when clinics were open 70 hours a week. During her 22 years of service, 320,000 pints of blood were collected.

During the Bowness Flood, in 1950, Gertrude went out with the fire department wagons at 1 a.m. For long hours she worked, helping rescue residents of Lowery Gardens caught by the swirling waters. In 1970, she was honoured with a 'Recognition' banquet, with tributes, gifts, and a car. In 1974, Gertrude was appointed a member of the Order of Canada.

# Ethel Knight Wilson 1902-1983

**Edmonton politician and community worker, Ethel Knight Wilson was the second woman in Alberta to be named a cabinet minister in the government. That happened in 1962 when Social Credit premier Ernest Manning named her a minister without portfolio. He could have named her a minister of labour for that's where her heart was – with blue collar workers, union members, the unemployed, the employed poor, working mothers, and low income families.**

It was while she was working to support her own family that Ethel became active and vocal in the labour movement. That led to municipal politics, where she served on Edmonton City Council from 1952 to 1966, and to provincial politics, where she served from 1959 to 1971. Always, Ethel spoke up for the 'little guy or girl' and in 1967 was responsible for the passage of Bill 86 in the legislature, a bill that established a Women's Bureau of Culture and Information. Out of that initiative came Hilltop House, a shelter and educational centre for destitute women. Ethel's community work also included service on the library board, the board of the Royal Alexandra hospital, the Health Board, the Recreation Commission, the Greater Edmonton Foundation, the Business and Professional Women's Club, and the Pentecostal Church.

# Helen Beny Gibson, C.M.  1902-1993

**Helen Beny Gibson combined a political career with more than 40 years of community service in Medicine Hat.**

Born in New York, Helen came to an Irvine homestead with her family in 1904. She was educated at local schools, at Mount Royal College in Calgary, and at the University of Alberta. She married Ross Gibson, a Calgary dentist, in 1929 and raised three children. Almost as soon as the family moved to Medicine Hat, Irene was involved in community and political activities. She served on the Separate School Board for two years and was a city alderman for 17 years. She represented the city on provincial and national organizations, primarily in the health and welfare fields.

Helen was a member of the Alberta chapter of the Muscular Dystrophy Association of Canada and a regional vice-president for years. She wrote *Thou Art My Only Hope,* the story of her son's struggle with the disease. She was also on the University of Calgary Senate for six years, served a two-year term on the Citizens Advisory Board to the Ministry of Education, and was a talented water colourist who had her own show. In 1973, Irene was named a member of the Order of Canada.

# Gertrude Hall  (died in 1960)

**Gertrude Hall took over as director of both the nursing school and nursing services at Calgary General Hospital in 1952. As one of the leaders in the Canadian nursing field, she immediately set about turning each into the best they could be.**

Gertrude brought many new ideas to Calgary General and made changes that directly affected the lives of the student nurses. She worked to free the students from overwhelming duty responsibilities so that they would have more time available for planned learning sessions. She revised and reorganized the nursing curriculum, grouped the teachers into a faculty unit, and doubled their number.

For the next eight years, Calgary General underwent dramatic expansion, and Gertrude provided expert leadership in nursing services, while taking care of the nursing students' needs. Gertrude died suddenly in 1960. Ten years later Gertrude M. Hall Auditorium opened at the hospital, and a trust fund was established in her name. The first Gertrude Hall Memorial Scholarship was awarded in 1974.

# Euphemia 'Betty' McNaught (born 1902)

**The McNaught family knew they had an artist in their midst when five-year-old Betty was able to draw anatomically correct – and funny – sketches of her older sisters.**

But it wasn't until she had finished high school in Beaverlodge in the Peace River country that Betty was able to take her talent to the next level. At the Ontario College of Art (OCA), she met and was guided by several members of Canada's Group of Seven: Arthur Lismer, J.E.H. MacDonald, and Lawren Harris. They helped her to realize the beauty of the north country. With a degree from OCA, Betty taught art in Calgary and Whitby, Ontario, but always she missed the north. So she went back to Beaverlodge, where she lived, painted, and taught art for the rest of her life.

In 1954, when the Alberta government bought eight paintings from Alberta artists as the basis for a permanent provincial art collection, Betty's *Edson Trail Days* was one of those selected. From then on, her art was in great demand, especially the pieces she did on the Alaska Highway, the Monkman Pass, and horses. Horses were a favorite subject, often part of the bronze sculptures she has done as well.

# Mary Percy Jackson (born 1904)

**When Dr. Mary Percy came to Alberta in 1929 as provincial district doctor for the Manning area, it was mainly wilderness, and she travelled on foot, by saddle horse, by wagon, by sleigh, and by dogsled to reach her patients.**

A native of England, she had graduated from the University of Birmingham with degrees in medicine and surgery. Reaching the Battle River in July, she set up residence and a practice in the infirmary that had been provided for her. She described it as, "a palatial shack, 14 feet by 20, (it was) divided into three rooms: a kitchen, scullery, and waiting room for patients; a bedroom/dispensary; and, a consulting-treatment room barely large enough for a patient and myself." Mary was the only doctor in the area, with the nearest hospital 84 miles to the south.

In 1931 she married Frank Jackson and went to Keg River, adding farm wife and mother to her medical duties. She fought arduous battles against rabies, a major hazard in the north, and to eradicate tuberculosis (TB), a killer disease among the native population. The last TB victim of the area died in 1952. Dr. Jackson retired in 1974 after 45 years of dedicated service to the people of northern Alberta.

71

# Mary Bowlen Mooney  1905-1987

**Mary Bowlen Mooney was wife, mother, community worker, all the expected roles for women, but her role as daughter took on extra glitter when her father became Lieutenant-Governor of Alberta.**

After her mother died, Mary became her father's official hostess and was known in official circles as 'Lady To His Honor the Lieutenant Governor.' As such, she accompanied her father, John James Bowlen, to the Coronation of Queen Elizabeth II in 1953, and then presided over the dinner table when royalty and other notables returned the visit.

With some influence behind her, Mary was able to forward the cause of the arts, her first love. In 1957, for example, she helped bring the Dominion Drama Festival to Edmonton as part of the Jubilee Auditorium's debut. She was on the festival board for 15 years. She was also president of the Women's Theatre Guild and a director of Citadel Theatre, all of which led to an honorary degree from the University of Alberta in 1969.

Before moving into the limelight in Edmonton, Mary was director of household economics for Calgary Separate Schools and national officer for the Pi Beta Phi, one of the first women's fraternities in Canada.

# Mary Cross Dover, O.B.E, C.M.  1905-1994

**Mary Cross Dover led at least four lives: young socialite, army lieutenant-colonel, local politician and community worker, and horticulturist.**

Granddaughter of Colonel J.F. Macleod, who issued the 1875 order to build the first fort at Calgary, Mary was the daughter of A.E. Cross, a successful rancher, businessman, and one of the original founders of the Calgary Stampede. Her early life was that of the beautiful young socialite, and then during the 1930s she married and became mother to a son. In 1941, she joined the Canadian Women's Army Corps (CWAC) and was promoted to lieutenant-colonel, commanding Canada's largest CWAC centre at Kitchener, Ontario. She was rewarded for her outstanding service with the Order of the British Empire in 1946.

During the 1950s and 1960s Mary served two terms as alderman, was a member of a hospital board, the District Planning Commission, and the Parks, Lands and Grants Committee. She served the Calgary Exhibition and Stampede Committee for seven years. Mary, who received the Order of Canada in 1974, also volunteered for causes such as the Red Cross and the Calgary Philharmonic. She pursued her horticultural interest by developing her Millarville garden.

# Elsie Park Gowan 1905-1999

**Elsie Park Gowan wrote plays for radio. She wrote plays for the theatre. She wrote plays for historical pageants. She adjudicated plays. She taught the art of playwriting. She even acted in plays now and then. In other words, the play was definitely the thing for Elsie.**

Born in Scotland, she came with her folks to Alberta in 1912. By her 17th birthday, she had finished her training and was out teaching in rural schools. Eventually, she finished a history degree with honors at the University of Alberta. That history degree came in handy forevermore because she chose mostly historical subjects for her productions. For example, *A Pageant of the Plains,* a commemoration of the signing of Treaty No. 6 with the Cree nations, was produced on Dried Meat Hill near Camrose and involved dozens of actors, horses, costumes, musicians, and technicians. It also drew an audience of some 5,000 people.

Elsie did two other major 'historamas' – one called *The Jasper Story,* which was produced outdoors at Jasper National Park, and *Who Builds A City,* which was a salute to the pioneers of Edmonton.

# Wilma Swinarton Hansen 1905-1999

**Wilma Swinarton Hansen believed that parents and teachers had to work together to build the best educational system possible. To that end, she joined the Home and School Association (HSA) as soon as her children were in school, and she moved steadily through the ranks to become an executive member of the Calgary Council of HSA, the Alberta Federation, and the Canadian Federation.**

She visited almost every part of Alberta for Home and School, edited the newsletter, organized workshops in leadership and served on committees and councils. A member of the Calgary Public School Board from 1961 to 1967, Wilma expanded her vision to include a university for Calgary and to that end served as chairman of the University Committee between 1963 and 1966. That contribution was recognized with an honourary degree from the University of Calgary in 1969.

Wilma was one of 300 persons from across Canada invited to Ottawa for the first conference of the Vanier Institute of the Family and later became one of its 100 members-at-large. In 1985, a Calgary school was named for her, the Wilma Hansen Junior High School.

# Gertrude Amies Laing, O.C.  (born 1905)

**Few Albertans knew the name Gertrude Laing until in 1963 she was appointed the only woman member of the Royal Commission on Bilingualism and Biculturalism (B&B), the controversial government panel that studied and came up with recommendations concerning the French and English solitudes in Canada.**

As it turned out, Calgary's own Gertrude had spoken and studied French both in Winnipeg and Paris. She was a natural for the job, and once the B&B commission was over, she co-wrote a book on Canada's two founding nations with French Canadian journalist Solange Chaput Rolland. The book was called *Face to Face*.

Gertrude moved with her husband and two sons from Winnipeg to Calgary in 1952 and did volunteer work in the areas of social service and the arts. The former led to work with the United Nations, the latter to chairmanship of the Canada Council. Her first honourary degree came from the University of Calgary in 1973. The rest came from the University of British Columbia in 1977, the University of Ottawa in 1978, and the University of Manitoba in 1980. She was named an officer of the Order of Canada in 1972

# Catharine Robb Whyte 1906-1979

**Catharine Whyte, artist and resident of Banff, was in love with the Rockies. With her husband, Peter, she painted, hiked, skied, and climbed the mountains. Pleasure in their surroundings led the couple to work to preserve the art and history of the area.**

In 1958 they created the Wa-Che-Yo-Cha-Pa Foundation, later renamed the Peter and Catharine Whyte Foundation. Catharine directed the foundation which supported projects that benefitted every aspect of Banff's community life, among others the beautiful building that houses the Banff Library, the Peter Whyte Gallery, and the Archives of the Canadian Rockies.

Catharine also personally funded various Stoney enterprises and countless projects in the areas of art, natural science, and parks and conservation. She found time to travel, visiting the Himalayas, sketching in Canada's Arctic, and touring the Soviet Union. She also kept permanent open house, serving tea to the steady stream of guests who visited her log home beside the gallery. Catharine's contribution to the cultural life, not only of Banff but also of Alberta as a whole, was recognized through many honours. Her favourite was from the Stoney, who made her an honorary Stoney, with the name Princess White Shield.

# Alice Baird Donahue  1906-1988

**After teaching for 11 years in small towns, Alice Baird left the uneventful life for the hardships of teaching in northern Alberta, where there was an acute shortage of teachers**

Marrying William Donahue in 1937, Alice moved to the Athabasca area, where the population was scattered and isolated. Although she hadn't planned to teach after marriage, she did when the need for teachers pressed her into service. At Assineau, she boarded with a family of 10 and lived on a diet of fish. Once, her room was furnished with "three blocks of wood, two for seats and one for the washstand."

Along with mosquitoes, flies, and bedbugs, Alice endured unpredictable salary arrangements. Sometimes she wasn't paid at all. Other times her pay came at the end of the year, usually discounted, or she was paid in installments. One position required her to cross the Athabasca River daily: "In the spring, when the ice was breaking up, and in the fall, when the ice was coming down, I had to cross in a cage. To me that was always a fearful time for we had to pass over the seething masses of ice that were turning and grinding against one another." Despite the hardships, Alice taught 46 years in the north.

# Eva Adeline Reid  1906-1989

**When the *Calgary Albertan* turned 78 years old, Eva Reid had been reporting, editing, or writing a column for 44 years of its existence.**

Born in Ontario, she came to Alberta with her parents in 1912. She completed high school there and then business courses at Mount Royal College. She said she "stumbled" into newspaper writing in the Depression and never stopped. Eva was one of the first women to cover the Calgary law courts, and she stayed on the beat for 20 years. She also served as the paper's provincial editor and its women's editor. Her last 20 years were spent writing her popular column, *Eavesdrop with Eva Reid.*

Eva was a vice-president with the Canadian Women's Press Club (CWPC), president of the Calgary branch, and a branch director. In 1971 she was named dean of newspaper women in Alberta at a CWPC ceremony. In 1976 she was named Woman of the Year by the Altrusa Club. In 1979 Eva was named Woman of the Year in the business and professional category, one of six Calgary women the Young Women's Christian Association named to celebrate 50 years of the Famous 5's success in having Canadian women formally recognized as 'persons'.

# Mona Stuart Sparling 1906-1992

**Camrose gained a particularly active citizen when Mona Stuart Sparling moved to town in 1958.**

Mona arrived when her husband, Col. Laurence Sparling, was appointed magistrate. She came with an abiding interest in community affairs and Canadian history and set to work. She organized Red Cross clinics and drives, became membership chairman of the Overture Concert Association, and by 1962 was elected to the local council. Mona was the first woman on council, and she served for 12 years.

She was also the first woman appointed to the executive of the Alberta Urban Municipalities Association. She served for nine years and became the first woman president in 1973. Mona was a member of the board of directors of the Canadian Federation of Mayors and Municipalities. Mona's interest in history led her to the Camrose and District Museum Society. She was an active member and an avid collector of artifacts. In 1973 she was elected to the Council of the Alberta Museum Association, serving as president in 1974. That same year she was also named to the board of governors of the Glenbow Museum in Calgary. Mona was Camrose's citizen of the year in 1974.

# Anne Svekia Porozni

**Daughter of Romanian immigrants, Anne Svekia Porozni is another woman who helped build an Alberta Master Farm.**

Anne came to Alberta as a child and was raised by parents devoted to the Romanian Orthodox church. She worshipped at a Boian church they helped build. In 1926, Anne married John Porozni. Two years later, they inherited John's family farm, a quarter-section with a $2,000 mortgage and a 14 x 18 foot log cabin. By 1951, when the Porozni farm was named a Master Farm, they had one and a half sections, herds of animals, and a modern seven-room home.

From the beginning, Anne did every kind of work on the farm: housework, milking cows, keeping a big garden, raising chickens, helping cut and stook grain, nothing was too much for her willing hands and heart. Gradually, the mortgage was paid off. Another quarter section of land was purchased and cleared, just as the Depression hit. In spite of the economic woes, the couple tried new machinery, products, and ideas, improving their herds, grain yields, and farming practice. With four sons and one daughter, Anne found time for community service.

# Louise Vogel Johnston  (born 1906)

**Louise Johnston, a member of the Alberta Agriculture Hall of Fame, is representative of the many Alberta farm women who dedicate themselves to leadership and service through women's farm organizations.**

Louise came to Alberta as a baby, grew up on a ranch at Carstairs, and taught in rural schools for five years.  She married Russel Johnston and lived in the Helmsdale district, becoming actively involved with the United Farm Women of Alberta (UFWA).  The UFWA is concerned with social issues, especially related to women and children: education, health and welfare, and the status of women.  Directors and presidents run committees to study and make proposals on the issues.  In her 18 years as a director, beginning in 1946, Louise prepared briefs on topics such as the need for a national health plan, fairer divorce laws for women, and education.  In education, she drafted and presented proposals to various Royal Commissions, and, between 1967 and 1971, served  on the senate of the University of Calgary.

From 1963 to 1967 Louise was UFWA president, taking on national and international tasks, as a delegate to conferences in Quebec and Ireland.

# Chito Kimura

**Knowing isolation, loneliness, and homesickness were recurrent themes in the lives of Western newcomers, especially those who were non-English speaking, Chito Kimura, a newcomer herself, thought of a remedy to ease the despair of her countrymen.**

"I knew a few Japanese people in British Columbia who could not speak any English and who were homesick. I began teaching Japanese dancing to these older people; I hoped to change their feelings of loneliness of Canada. I was successful as they were very happy to start this dancing which brought them closer to their homeland."

In 1942 Chito and her husband came to Coaldale, Alberta where they ran a confectionery store.  What began as a remedy for homesickness became a lifetime vocation of promoting and preserving Japanese culture.  Chito continued to teach dancing, always on a voluntary basis.  She shared her talents with students in school and church groups, including religious ceremonies at six Buddhist churches.  As well, she produced dolls clothed in traditional styles and taught Japanese drama.  Her husband Takeo directed the plays and organized the music for her dances.

# Ethel Watson Taylor  1908-1989

**Ethel Taylor, once hesitant even to talk on the phone, became Red Deer's first woman alderman in 1961 and served continuously for 14 years.** Her interest in community affairs increased with experience in Canadian Girls In Training, Women's Institute, Local Council of Women, and the Alberta Federation of Home and School Associations.

Born in Southern Rhodesia, Ethel was the eldest of five children of a Canadian soldier who married overseas during the Boer War. The family stayed briefly in England before coming in 1912 to Fort Macleod to stay with Ethel's pioneering grandparents. Her parents died in Camrose when Ethel was young. Ethel married a teacher, L.H. Taylor, a member of a pioneering family in the Pincher Creek area.

A diligent community worker, Ethel was a founding member of the Alberta and Red Deer councils on aging, and strongly supported the arts, Red Deer College, the social planning council, and many other organizations. She also served six years on the University of Alberta Senate. Among her many honours were the Centennial Award in 1967, an Alberta Achievement Award for Service in 1975, and Citizen of the Year for Red Deer in 1977.

# Winnifred Parker Stewart  1908-1990

**Duncan Parker Stewart was born in 1934 and that changed everything for his mother, Winnifred Parker Stewart. The boy was a Downs Syndrome baby back in the days when mentally challenged children were expected to stay out of sight, out of mind, in institutions.**

Winnifred Stewart, a trained nurse and determined mother, decided instead to keep her son at home and teach him as much as possible. She researched everything she could find about mental retardation and over the years devised successful teaching methods to help Parker lead a normal life. In 1953, she took her tried and true teaching methods and became the principal of a school for mentally handicapped children. The next year, she went to bat for the children in Alberta's legislature when she argued for the need for financial support for schools like hers. Some support followed then; more and more came through the years. More and more organizations, also with Winnifred's guidance, took on the challenge of special needs children as well.

Many honours came Winnifred's way, none as rewarding as the fact that son Parker did indeed learn and was a capable member of society.

# Christine MacKenzie Meikle, C.M. 1908-1997

**Christine Meikle's devotion to the cause of educating children with learning handicaps covered the continuum, from the development of special schools for the children to the integration of the schools into the Calgary school system.**

Christine moved to Canada from Scotland in 1929 and began her education work in 1952 when she founded the Calgary Association for Retarded Children. She helped found the Alberta Association in 1954, and the Canadian Association in 1956. Classes were held in her home, church basements, and a house provided by the Junior League, before an eight-room school was opened in 1957. The Christine Meikle school was a first in Canada. A second school and an activity center followed.

By 1969, educational philosophy had changed and the two schools and activity center were integrated into the Calgary school system. Christine continued as supervisor. She was named to the board when the Vocational Rehabilitation and Research Institute began operating in cooperation with the University of Calgary. In 1973, Christine was appointed a member of the Order of Canada. Christine and her husband William were the parents of eight children.

# Laura Margaret Attrux 1909-1987

**Laura Attrux, a highly qualified obstetrical nurse with a diploma in public nursing, delivered 1,031 babies with no maternal deaths, during 35 years of service to mothers and infants.**

With six years' experience as obstetrical supervisor at Holy Cross Hospital, Calgary, Laura applied for a position as district nurse in 1939. She recalled, "Within a week I was off to my first district, which was Valleyview. My closest medical and hospital facilities were at High Prairie, 50 miles away, a dirt road as the only source of communication."

The District Nursing Service provided medical aid to remote communities. To people in the communities the district nurse was an all encompassing hero figure, serving as nurse, doctor, dentist, counsellor, social worker, community leader and, above all, friend. The nurses encountered many difficulties – including below-zero temperatures and primitive housing facilities – but the greatest was transportation. Roads, if they existed, were in poor condition; dog teams were used in winter, wagons at other times. In 1967, at age 60, Laura improved her transportation situation by qualifying for a private pilot's licence and buying her own plane, a 1967 Cessna 150. Laura retired in 1974.

*I was chosen in 1954 at ✦✦✦ of A. P Health to go to her in Slave Lake for a months field work, Wonderful!*

79

# Mary Elizabeth Munn  1909-1991

**By May 1973, Mary Elizabeth Munn had earned a doctorate in musical arts from the University of Boston, the first blind woman in the world to be so distinguished. Mary believed her achievement would help open the field to other blind people and encourage funding organizations to sponsor blind students.**

Mary never let her handicap be an obstacle to the things she wanted to do: dancing, skating, riding, and hiking. To get her doctorate, she worked 17 hours a day, seven days a week for 16 months, often with as many as five readers supplying her with information. She completed the program eight months early.

Mary studied at the Royal Academy of Music, London and at the Tobias Matthay school, where she obtained her teacher's certificate. Her first concert in London launched a 20-year career in which she performed across North America and in Europe. During World War II, she was a member of the Women's Ambulance Corps in Vancouver, serving as switchboard operator and filing clerk. In 1953, having given up concert work, Mary came to Calgary to begin a teaching career at the Calgary Conservatory of Music.

# Ivy McAfee Taylor

**Teacher Ivy McAfee Taylor was the first woman named to the Alberta Agricultural Hall of Fame.**

Belfast-born but Edmonton-raised, Ivy went to Camrose Normal School and taught at Mayerthorpe and Edgerton. After she married Walter Taylor, she became increasingly involved in the farm organizations and politics. She was already a member of the United Farm Women of Alberta (UFWA), and she went on to be a director and then president. She was an executive member of the Farmers Union of Alberta and a member of the Interprovincial Farm Union Council.

After moving to Wainwright, Ivy was elected to the town council and was chairman of the property committee for more than a decade. She was chairman of the Wainwright General and Auxiliary Hospital Board and chairman of the Battle River Foundation Board, among numerous other local roles. She was a member of the Alberta Royal Commission on Education in the 1950s and of the Alberta Colleges Commission in the early 1970s. In 1972, she was appointed to the Alberta Agricultural Hall of Fame, the first woman so honoured. Ivy and Walter raised two children.

# Barbara Harvey Leighton (died in 1986)

**In 1974, Barbara Leighton established Calgary's Leighton Foundation, a non-profit organization that provides year-round instruction to students of all ages, in painting, sculpture, weaving, batik, silk-screening, jewelry-making, ceramics, and metalwork.** In 1935 Barbara, an art student, married her teacher, A.C. Leighton, an internationally known landscape painter. She spent 30 years sharing his unconventional and widely travelled life. After he died in 1965, Barbara returned to art college to resume her long-abandoned artistic pursuits. Studying fabrics and metalwork, she won art scholarships two years in a row, and graduated in 1969.

After working in her chosen media and making prints of her husband's work, Barbara decided to make her skills available to others. She opened her home, with its spectacular view of the Rockies, as an art centre where people could come for lessons in arts and crafts. Before long, a nearby schoolhouse was purchased to accommodate the growing number of students and other buildings - a weaving studio, a pottery studio and a woodworking shop - were added. The Leighton Centre became an informal art gallery where works of well-known and promising artists of Alberta are displayed.

# Ellen Lowe Armstrong 1910-1975

**When Ellen Lowe from Toronto married Clarence Armstrong, a farmer from Hussar, Alberta, she noticed that rural concerns didn't often make it onto local and national radio and television programs. That didn't seem fair to her, so she decided to do something about the imbalance.**

A licensed amateur radio operator, she taped a weekly news program that was rebroadcast on seven Alberta radio stations. Soon she was being asked to speak about farming subjects on radio programs across Canada. The CBC heard her and asked her to serve as a director from 1958 to 1965, during which time she managed to get *This Business of Farming* on television.

Ellen worked with the Farm Women's Union of Alberta and the Federations of Agriculture, but her social activism didn't stop with farming issues. She served with the Alberta Council on Child Welfare, the Alberta Safety Council, the provincial Mental Health Association, and Business and Professional Women's Clubs. She worked to have family courts set up in Alberta, a school of social work established in the province, divorce laws revised, more rural health units opened, and old age pensions improved.

81

# Leona Flegal Paterson

It was a natural for Leona Flegal Paterson. Professionally trained in speech arts and drama and teaching of the same at Mount Royal College in Calgary, she said to the administration one day, "We should offer a course in radio broadcasting." And so it was that Mount Royal became the first college in western Canada to offer broadcasting as a credit course.

The course now covers television and radio and is a major faculty within the college, a long way from its humble beginnings with a home turntable and some borrowed records. When Mount Royal moved from its downtown location to the present much-larger campus in 1972, Leona became the director of the conservatory of music and speech arts. Five years later when she retired, she had been with the college 31 years, an achievement they honored with a theatre arts scholarship in her name.

Her speech arts also took her across Canada as adjudicator and teacher at numerous speech and drama festivals. Closer to home, Leona served for many summers as a member of the faculty of the Banff School of Fine Arts. She also sponsored a special kindergarten for hearing impaired children.

# Pearl Edmanson Borgal  1911-1993

Sports defined Pearl Borgal's life, first as a participant in just about any sport you can name – hockey, basketball, swimming, golfing, and speed skating, then as a swimming and riding coach, then as an organizer of girls' rodeo, then as a broadcaster. Her daily sports program on CKXL radio in Calgary is said to have been the first in Canada hosted by a woman.

Pearl's community involvement didn't stop with sports, however. In Lethbridge, she was active in the organizing of the first Young Women's Christian Association and Victorian Order of Nurses chapters. She also worked to have a senior citizen's lodge built, was a member of the town planning commission, and was active in the Home and School Association. For Alberta's 50th anniversary, she organized and served as parade marshal for an all women's parade. After moving back to Calgary, she added Miles for Millions and Oxfam to her list of community involvement.

In the 1960s, Pearl organized the first all-girls rodeos and subsequently became the founding director of the Canadian Girls Rodeo Association. At the same time as she wrote and broadcast news about sports, she became an award-winning member of the Canadian Women's Press Club.

# Helen Griffith Wylie McArthur, O.C.   (died in 1974)

**Helen McArthur was Canada's Florence Nightingale. In fact, she won an award by that name in 1957, the highest international nursing award that the Red Cross can bestow. It was given in recognition of her 25 years as national director of nursing.**

With a bachelor's of science in public health nursing degree from the University of Alberta in 1934 and a master's degree in supervision and teaching from Columbia University, Helen became director of the School of Nursing, University of Alberta. Then she was head of public health nursing for the province for three years. She joined the Canadian Red Cross Society and served in Korea rebuilding the infrastructure of public health. Onward and upward she went, chairing a nursing advisory committee in Geneva, Switzerland and serving on an International Council of Nurses. Back in Canada, she was president of the Canadian Nurses Association and the Ontario College of Nurses.

No wonder the University of Alberta gave Stettler-born Helen an honourary degree in 1964. She was one of their own. And no wonder the powers-that-be appointed her an officer of the Order of Canada in 1971. She married Dr. William Watson in 1971.

# Alison Jackson  1912-1987

**An idea Alison Jackson had on a walk home for lunch in 1956 launched a project which captured the history of Calgary and southern Alberta.**

Alison hated to see the Pat Burns residence destroyed, so she decided that lunch hour to take a picture of it. And then she decided to take a picture of Col. James Macleod's house. That was the beginning of her project to preserve pictures of buildings of historic interest before time or progress destroyed them. By 1980 Alison had approximately 1,500 photographs of buildings from across southern Alberta. Each picture carefully documented the building, and Alison recorded anecdotes about the people who lived and worked in them.

Alison was raised in Calgary. She attended Calgary Normal School and Mount Royal College prior to earning a bachelor's degree, a bachelor's of library science degree, and a master's of library science degree from the universities of Alberta, Washington, and Michigan. She was on staff at the Calgary Public Library for nearly 34 years, 17 years as head of the cataloguing. Alison had another special interest – the collecting of dolls, remarkable for age, manufacture, or distinctive dress. She carefully recorded each doll's history.

# Sara Lehn Harder  (born 1912)

**Sara Lehn Harder taught school for 40 years, thus making a difference to hundreds of young lives. But when she moved to northern Alberta in 1955 to teach in the two-roomed schoolhouse at Buffalo Head Prairie School, she made a difference to the whole community.**

It was a Mennonite community, and many of the pioneers in the area spoke Low German only. Sara was bilingual; she grew up in the Ukraine and spoke German and then learned English when her family emigrated to Canada in 1926. She was able to negotiate conflicts that arose between the Mennonite community and Alberta school authorities. Eventually, she and the principal were able to work out a curriculum that suited both the independent Mennonites and the Department of Education.

Trained at Saskatoon Normal School, she worked for 13 years in rural schools in Saskatchewan and then seven years in a Mennonite Bible School. While in the north, she managed to complete her bachelor's of education degree through the University of Alberta. As well, Sara planted a garden and started handicraft classes for young people, both activities engendering trust in the remote community. In 1964, she married fellow teacher John Harder.

# Anne Campbell, C.M.  (born 1912)

**The motto, 'Blessed is a world that sings, Gentle are its songs,' was written on the program of the 1974 music festival and competition in Wales known as the Eisteddfod. Anne Campbell couldn't have agreed more. She was there with the Anne Campbell Singers, a girls' choir from Lethbridge, and she hoped to win, just as they had in 1968 when they were the first Canadian choir to win a first in the prestigious international contest.**

The Anne Campbell Singers began as a single church choir but evolved into several interdenominational groups that sang everything from sacred music to folk songs to early madrigals. Winning awards at every turn, they were invited to perform at Canada's Expo in 1967 and at Expo 1970.

Born and raised in Saskatchewan, Anne was singing by the age of seven and conducting a senior choir by age 14. After advanced piano and singing classes in Saskatoon, she took her choral training at the Banff School of Fine Arts. As well as conducting her various choirs, she taught music and adjudicated music festivals. Anne has been honoured with membership in the Order of Canada in 1976 and as Lethbridge Young Women's Christian Association Woman of the Year in 1980.

# Margaret Smith Parsons  1913-1984

**Margaret Smith was a 'first lady' in school when she obtained first-class honours in every one of 36 subjects she took in grades 9 to 12 in Calgary.** Years later, as Margaret Smith Parsons of Red Deer, she was actually named 'First Lady in Education in Alberta, 1966' by the Council of School Administrators, not for her marks but for her service as a school and college trustee.

By then, she had five children, and her focus had changed from her own marks to those of young people in Red Deer and Alberta. Margaret started as a member of Home and School. She moved on to the Red Deer Public School Board as a trustee and chairman from 1955 to 1966. Concurrently, she served as an executive member of the Alberta School Trustees Association.

Red Deer had no post-secondary educational facilities in the 1950s, so Margaret added that to her agenda. In 1963, the Red Deer Junior College opened with Margaret on both the local college board and the Alberta Association of College Administration. In 1968, she turned to municipal politics and won a seat as alderman. She got to be 'first lady' again when she was named 1972 Red Deer Citizen of the Year.

# Helen Reynolds Belyea, O.C.  1913–1986

**Throughout her life, Helen Reynolds Belyea broke new ground. In 1936 Helen moved from Saint John, New Brunswick to Chicago where she received her doctorate in geology from Northwestern University. Following three years of teaching and two years as a lieutenant in the Women's Royal Canadian Navy Service during World War II, she joined the Geological Survey of Canada. She was transferred to Calgary to help open an office there.**

Helen carried out research into the oil-bearing Devonian system at the Institute of Sedimentary and Petroleum Geology from 1950 to 1975. She co-chaired the first International Devonian Symposium held in Calgary in 1967. She participated in the National Research Council's 1969 exchange of scientists and spent four weeks lecturing in France. Her work won her many honours: officer of the Order of Canada in 1976, fellow of the Royal Society of Canada (1964), honourary member of the Canadian Society of Petroleum Geologists, and several honourary degrees.

Helen was a member of the Calgary Continuing Arts Association, the Women's League of the Calgary Philharmonic, and associate director of the Calgary Zoological Society.

# Violet Louise Archer  (born 1913)

**Violet Archer's list of music honours, achieved through composing and gifted leadership to many young composers, is lengthy.  Much of the musical activity in Edmonton and throughout Alberta is the result of her imaginative efforts.**

Montreal-born, Violet was a student and later a professor at McGill University.  Her music, atonal and 20th century, is praised by critics for expressing uniquely the "vastness and newness" of Canada.  Citing religion as "a deeply personal thing with me," she composed an acclaimed *Cantata Sacra*.  She was inspired by the music of Hindemith and Bartok, and herself composed chamber music, orchestral and choral works, music for cello and piano, clarinet and piano, a brass quintet, even music for carillon.  She was the first to present electronic music in Alberta, at the 1964 convention of the Alberta Registered Music Teachers' Association, Banff.

Violet headed the theory and composition department at the University of Alberta from 1962 to 1978, providing dynamic leadership to its young composers.  Her awards include a Yale University citation for distinguished service, 1968 and a McGill honourary doctor of music degree, 1971.

# Maria Agopsowicz Chrzanowski  (born 1913)

**Maria Agopsowicz Chrzanowski devoted more than 40 years to teaching Polish at a Saturday school in Edmonton.  She directed a Polish program on CKUA radio for years and worked with the Friends of Canadian Polish Youth, an auxiliary to scouts and guides.**

Trained as a teacher in Lvov, Maria spent World War II in occupied Poland taking care of her young son.  Her husband Jan had left the country in 1939 to fight with a Polish unit in  Britain, and the next year her parents were sent to Siberia, where they disappeared.

Maria and Jan were reunited in England in 1947, and the family came to Edmonton in 1948.  A daughter was born there.  In 1956, Maria began teaching Polish on Saturdays at the Henryk Sienkiewicz School.  By 1963, she was the school's principal.  She taught Polish for many years, but that was not her only community activity.  Maria worked on cancer campaigns for 18 years, was a past president of the Polish Canadian Women's Federation, and was in charge of Polish programs on CKUA for more than 15 years.  In 1975 she received a gold badge of merit from the Canadian Polish Congress and a gold cross of merit from the Polish government in exile in London, England.

# Jean Patterson Hoare (born in 1914)

**Jean Patterson Hoare, originator, owner, manager, and chef of Claresholm's famed Flying N Restaurant, never took a formal cooking lesson in her life. Yet she managed to turn not one but two unlikely locations into restaurant successes.**

Easterners Jean and Stanley Hoare were novices when they came west after World War II. Their farm four miles out of Claresholm offered few conveniences and many hardships – fire, flood, drought, and high wind. The couple survived with the help of neighbours and raised two children. Jean's childhood interest in cooking led her to open the Driftwood Room at the ranch in 1956. The restaurant was located at the end of a gravel road, but customers from Calgary and Lethbridge found it, thanks to Jean's warm hospitality and good food. Her next location, a former Royal Canadian Army Service Corps supply depot near Claresholm, was not much easier to locate. But customers came in such numbers the restaurant eventually expanded to seat 300.

Jean was interested in pioneer history, and she started the Willow Creek Round Up, which led directly to the founding of the Willow Creek Historical Association. The round ups were annual events for 16 years.

# Ruby Ila Larson (born 1914)

**Ruby Ila Larson was hailed all over the world for her work as a wheat cytogeneticist, but very few in Alberta knew anything about her or her accomplishments. She was a scientist who toiled away at the Lethbridge Research Station, doing experiments with wheat chromosomes to see if they could be made resistant to sawfly, root rot, and mites, and if somehow they could fix their own nitrogen and be self-fertilizing. It's not the stuff of everyday conversation, but that's what Ruby did, and her efforts contributed greatly to the development of better wheat strains.**

She started as a schoolteacher in rural Saskatchewan, but one summer she took a course in biology, and she was hooked. Many courses later, she had her doctorate from the University of Missouri in genetics, cytology, entomolgy, and botany.

Ruby joined Agriculture Canada and worked first at the Swift Current Experimental Station and then in Lethbridge. She was honoured by the Genetic Society of Canada, the Entomological Institute of Canada, the Agricultural Institute of Canada, and the University of Lethbridge. She took her greatest pleasure in the science club she organized for the young people of Lethbridge.

# Olive Fimrite Stickney  (born 1914)

**A champion of rural living, Olive Fimrite Stickney learned about the hardships early and dedicated her life to the development of rural Alberta.**

Olive arrived in the Peace River district when she was two. Her widowed mother, Inga Alexandra Fimrite, brought the toddler and her two brothers to a Valhalla homestead in 1916. Olive's mother bartered washing, mending, and baking for farm help and taught her children how to plough and fix fences. A brother sold a prize heifer so Olive could go to high school. After Olive married Lewis Stickney in 1939, she moved to Hythe, where the couple farmed and raised five children.

By 1966, Olive was elected to the County of Grande Prairie Council, becoming only its second woman councillor. She represented Hythe district on council for 14 years and council on the health unit board, the further education council, and on the preventive social services unit. When she was re-elected in 1980, Olive also became chairman of the County Board of Education. One of her pet projects was housing for seniors in the Hythe district. As a result of her efforts, a 58-bed senior citizens home was built.

# Martha Palamarek Bielish  (born 1915)

**It took 50 years but Alberta finally got a woman Senator in 1979, when Martha Bielish from Warspite was named. Even though it was five Alberta women – known as the Famous 5 – who in 1929 made it possible for women to be called to Canada's upper house, it wasn't until Martha was named that Alberta women were finally represented.**

When she joined the local Women's Institute (WI) chapter in 1944, it was the beginning of Martha's public life. She was president of the provincial WI from 1965 to 1969, president of the Federated Women's Institute of Canada from 1976 to 1979, and Canadian vice president of the Associated Country Women of the World. She served or advised the Royal Commission on the Status of Women, Council on Aging, Human Rights Association, Consumer Association, Voice of Alberta Native Women, Cancer Society, and Canadian Council on Rural Development.

In 1980, Martha was inducted into the Alberta Agriculture Hall of Fame and in 1981, she received an honourary degree from the University of Calgary. Always, however, she describes herself simply as "homemaker and farmer's wife," titles that she believes are as important as any others she had.

# Ruth Peacock Gorman, O.C. (born 1915)

**Ruth Gorman, a well-known Calgary lawyer, has two other names: 'Mountain White Girl Eagle,' given her by the Stoney, and 'Morning Star,' her Cree name.**

That two native bands should honour her is not surprising; Ruth was volunteer legal advisor to Alberta's native people for 25 years, following in her father Colonel M.B. Peacock's footsteps defending native rights in court. Working with John Laurie, Ruth helped institute reforms to provide natives with civil rights and equal opportunities, including the Hobbema Case, a five-year battle that led to changes in the Indian Act and prepared the way for native peoples to get the vote.

Besides working in native affairs, Ruth has been legal advisor to the Local Council of Women for more than 30 years, helping bring about reforms ranging from getting skim milk legalized to changing the Dower Act. In 1951 she helped organize the Calgary Handicapped Society for Crippled Persons and was instrumental in developing a school and shop for training disabled people. In 1965, recognizing a need for regional publications, she became the founder, publisher, and editor of a small magazine, *My Golden West*. Among other honours, Ruth was named an officer of the Order of Canada in 1968.

# Margareta 'Gretta' Keenan Houseworth

**Gretta Houseworth made room in her Dimsdale home for one mother and her two children in 1955. Twenty-five years later she had fostered hundreds of children at the Grace Children's Home.**

Irish-born, Gretta came to Canada in 1931 to visit a sister. She fell in love with Alberta and stayed, marrying Roy Houseworth in Grande Prairie. The couple, who had two children, believed they had a calling to help children in need and opened their doors to a mother when she came asking for help in 1955. More than 325 homeless children followed that family to the home, approximately 10 miles from Grande Prairie, over the years. And others stayed temporarily while their mothers were hospitalized.

The Houseworths managed Grace Children's Home without much outside financial help. They housed from five to 25 children at any one time, running Grace as a home rather than an institution. The children were raised in a non-denominational Christian setting. When the couple's log cabin was destroyed by fire in 1960, a community campaign raised funds for them to re-build. Gretta was named Lady of the Year in Grande Prairie in 1974.

# Alison Seymour Vaness  (born 1915)

**School libraries inadvertently became the focus of Margaret Alison Seymour Vaness' working life.**

Alison was born in Fort Macleod, Alberta but received her early education in Calgary. She attended the Calgary Normal School and Commercial High School for teacher training and business education. She worked in the business world before beginning her teaching career at Westward Ho and Three Hills, Alberta in 1939.

She joined the staff of the Calgary Public School Board in 1945 and inaugurated a junior-high service jointly operated by the school and public library boards. In 1960 the Library Service Centre was established with Alison as supervisor of public school libraries. She influenced the development of standards of library service for Canadian schools. In 1967, the school board received the Encyclopedia Britannica Award for the most outstanding progress in library service of any city system in Canada.

Alison retired in 1980  and was elected a school board trustee, becoming vice-chairman. In 1972, she was awarded an honourary doctorate from the University of Calgary and earned an Alberta Achievement Award. In 1967 she earned a Centennial Medal.

# E. Jean Mackie   1916-1997

**Jean Mackie initiated Alberta's first two-year program for nurses in 1967 at Mount Royal College, Calgary. After a long and varied experience in nursing and nursing education, she became convinced that the apprenticeship method of training nurses was too limited in general education, particularly the behavioral sciences.**

Jean was born in Winnipeg, Manitoba and came to Alberta with her parents and brother to settle on a farm in the Beaverlodge area. Jean and a friend joined a group in 1937 attempting to forge through the bush and mountain to find a closer route to market on the British Columbia coast. After two summers' work they were forced to abandon the plan when war intervened. Jean graduated from the Royal Alexandra Hospital School of Nursing in Edmonton in 1944.

With an alumnae scholarship, Jean attended the University of Toronto and McGill University, obtaining a bachelor's degree from McGill in 1953. After teaching in Medicine Hat and Calgary, she went to the University of Washington for a master's degree in nursing education. Jean wrote *The First Decade, 1963-1973*, a history of the Mount Royal nursing program.

*Alex Monkman gathered a crew of Beaverlodge men to work on the Monkman Pass Highway. Jean & Chrissy Monkman cooked for the crew (4 men each year) using a stove on a flat rack!*

# Marjorie Montgomery Bowker   (born 1916)

**That girls should have a university education was not a commonly held belief in the 1930s, but Marjorie Montgomery got a law degree from the University of Alberta because her mother said so.**

Her mother didn't buy the argument that girls didn't need an education because they'd just get married anyway.  Mind you, once Marjorie was admitted to the bar, she did in fact get married to Wilbur Bowker, a fellow lawyer.  But she used her education to keep her husband's law practice going while he served in the war, and then once the three children were grown, she returned to the practice of law.

In 1965, the Alberta government appointed her to a committee studying adoption and child welfare, and a year later, she was appointed a family court judge in Edmonton, the first woman in Alberta to hold this position.  So many of the cases that came before her involved marriage breakdown that she studied and then recommended a system of marriage conciliation within the court, a project that attracted national interest.  International interest came her way in 1968 when she was asked to speak at a Women's University in Seoul, Korea.  There she received the honourary degree of doctor of laws.

# Ruth Carse  (born 1916)

**Ruth Carse turned a youthful dancing career into a lifetime of commitment to ballet in Alberta, in both teaching and choreography.**

After school and dance training in Edmonton, Ruth went to Toronto both to study and to perform with the Volkoff Canadian Ballet.  She moved on to New York, Chicago, and London always combining studying with a performing career.  She returned to Canada when the National Ballet was formed.  Then she went back to England, but her career there ended in injury.  Ruth became a teacher.  When she returned to Edmonton in 1954, her wealth of training, performing and teaching experience was put to good use.

For the next 21 years, Ruth founded, was artistic director, and led Dance Interlude, the forerunner of the Edmonton Ballet Company.  She opened the Albert Ballet Company School in 1970 and taught thousands of students the art of dance.  She also choreographed more than 45 works, including ballets for the company.  Ruth gave up her involvement with the company only to concentrate on the school and its students.  She was awarded an Alberta Achievement Award in 1976 and a Queen Elizabeth Silver Jubilee Medal in 1977.

# Violet Otter Crowchild  (born 1918)

**Violet Otter Crowchild lived all of her life on the Sarcee Reserve, although she did things differently from the time she was a child.**

Her parents, Oscar and Daisy Otter, believed in education, but Oscar did not want his children in residential schooling. The solution was that they were enrolled in day school and Oscar took them to and from class until they were old enough to manage on their own. Violet married Harold Crowchild and had seven children, one of whom died early. Violet also believed in education and encouraged her family to stay in school.

She went one step further, however, and became a school counsellor herself in the mid-1960s. She was one of the first two native counsellors hired by the Calgary Public School Board. Violet took courses at the University of Lethbridge to upgrade her qualifications, and was a school counsellor for more than 14 years. She also served on the Sarcee Development Company board, and on the reserve's land and education committees. She worked with Anglican Church women's organizations for more than 40 years, was a member of Homemakers for 20 years, and worked with local 4-H clubs.

# Martha Block Cohen, C.M.  (born 1920)

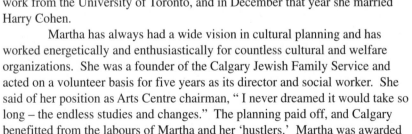

**When she was leading the campaign to build the Calgary Centre For the Performing Arts, Martha Cohen, fundraiser extraordinaire, described herself and her team to a *Calgary Herald* reporter: "We call ourselves the hustlers. We hustle money all over town."  By December 1981, Martha and her band of six volunteers had already raised $9.5 million for the centre.**

Born in Calgary, the only child of Rebecca and Peter Block, Martha was educated in Calgary and Toronto. In 1945 she obtained her diploma in social work from the University of Toronto, and in December that year she married Harry Cohen.

Martha has always had a wide vision in cultural planning and has worked energetically and enthusiastically for countless cultural and welfare organizations. She was a founder of the Calgary Jewish Family Service and acted on a volunteer basis for five years as its director and social worker. She said of her position as Arts Centre chairman, " I never dreamed it would take so long – the endless studies and changes." The planning paid off, and Calgary benefitted from the labours of Martha and her 'hustlers.' Martha was awarded an Order of Canada in 1975.

# Marie Plaizier

Marie Plaizier thought homemakers should have a break now and then – a retreat perhaps – especially those who lived in isolated rural areas in northern Alberta. A native of the Netherlands, she came to Canada in 1950 and moved directly with her husband to a farm near Peace River. Struggling to learn English and Canadian ways, she joined the local Women's Institute (WI) and found there a home.

By 1978, Marie was president of the provincial WI organization and a delegate to conferences of the Associated Country Women of the World. But back home, she was still worrying about the particular stresses brought about by fluctuating incomes, distances, isolation, and loneliness of rural women. Over and over she repeated the idea of Homemakers Retreats until finally in 1975, one was held in Falher. A great success, it was followed by more of the same, and the idea was incorporated as the Peace River Retreat Society.

Marie's other community involvement included the United Church, several provincial advisory committees dealing with further education, and the consortium responsible for setting up a university campus in Peace River.

# Helen Hunley (born 1920)

Helen Hunley was one of the few women in the farm implement business when she ran an implement and truck dealership in Rocky Mountain House in the 1960s. She was also one of the first women to hold a cabinet portfolio in Alberta government and the first woman to be the Lieutenant-Governor, 1985-1991.

A telephone operator after high school, Helen joined the Canadian Women's Army Corps during World War II. She served overseas and came home to help on the family farm for a year. Next she worked at the implement and truck dealership, buying it after nine years. She earned a journeyman's certificate as a partsman and held the local International Harvester franchise until 1968. From 1968 to 1971, she added an insurance business to the dealership.

Municipal politics were a part of her life in Rocky Mountain House. She served as town councillor for six years and mayor for five more. In 1971 she was elected to the Alberta legislature and appointed minister without portfolio. In 1973 she became Alberta's first solicitor general. In 1975, after re-election, Helen was appointed minister of social services. She retired in 1979. Outside of politics, Helen was active in community affairs, particularly with the Red Cross Society and the Boy Scouts.

# Flore Chretien Shaw

Before her marriage, Flore Chretien played in a seven piece band in the Lacombe area, played the organ in church, and played the piano at most community functions. When she married David Shaw in 1940 and moved to Berwyn in northern Alberta, she did all of the above plus gave music lessons to 40 to 50 pupils per week. Multiply that by the 59 years that she's been giving lessons, and you can see that Flore Shaw is the Music Woman of the North. She even played piano for 18 years for a weekly half-hour, live radio show on CKYL in Peace River.

Flore also belonged to and worked for the Home and School Association, the Women's Institute, the Legion Ladies Auxiliary, the Peace River Overture Association, and the Catholic Women's League. When she was elected to town council in 1967, the town quickly named her mayor for the next four years.

With money from her husband's estate, Flore established a fellowship for cancer research at the Cross Cancer Institute in Edmonton, an endowment fund for a master's of music program at the University of Alberta, and two annual awards for piano students in the north Peace country.

# Nora Gladstone Baldwin

For most Canadians in the 1930s, a trip to England was on par with flying to the moon, but in 1937 Nora Gladstone went to England as one of two native girls chosen from Canada to attend the coronation of King George V1.

It was a great honour, one that she earned by becoming the first Alberta native woman to complete her training as a nurse. On her return from England, Nora modeled the outfit she had worn at the Coronation for her people, and they in turn gave her the name Princess Ninaki. Nora's accomplishments encouraged other girls to stick with school and special training.

Nora was born on the Blood Reserve in southern Alberta, the daughter of Janie Healy and James Gladstone, later Senator Gladstone. When she completed her high school studies, she went to Toronto and Victoria for her nurse's training, specializing in the area of pediatrics. After marriage to Ed Baldwin, she continued to work with children in various hospitals on the west coast.

# Mary Barclay, C.M. (born 1901)
# Catherine Barclay 1902-1985

**One sister photographed flowers and trees in the mountains and collected rocks for her classroom. The other sister taught French and established student exchanges between France and Alberta. Together, they hiked the foothills and mountains west of Calgary and wished more people could afford to do the same.**

Then Catherine Barclay came home from a trip to Europe in 1931 and told her sister Mary about the hostels she had seen abroad. Why couldn't Canada have a system like that, she wondered. More people could afford to experience the mountains if they had inexpensive lodging. Why not, Mary agreed, and two years later, they set up the first hostel in Canada, a tent in a farmer's field near Bragg Creek, west of Calgary. For 25 cents a night, hikers could bunk down in the tent and save themselves a lot of money, not to mention wet clothes and frozen fingers. Thus was born the Canadian Youth Hostel Association, now a network of hundreds of less expensive lodging places across the country.

Both the sisters served on the boards and committees necessary for the organization, both continued to be hiking and outdoor enthusiasts throughout their long lives. But Catherine gradually spent more time on promoting the French language and culture in western Canada. It was she, for example, who founded the French program at the Banff School of Fine Arts. Mary then became chief spokesman for the hostelling movement. Yet they were always careful to credit one another for the accomplishment.

Both trained as teachers, Mary at the University of Chicago and the University of Toronto, Catherine at Sorbonne in Paris, Columbia in New York, and the University of Alberta. Mary retired in 1966, her sister a year later. Mary received an Order of Canada in 1987. In 1973 when the Calgary Jaycees named their annual Citizen of the Year, they had to prepare two citations and two awards. The citizen was, after all, the two Barclay sisters.

# Moretta 'Molly' Fenton Beall Reilly 1922-1980

**Recipient of the Amelia Earhart trophy and the first woman appointed Companion of the Order of Icarus, Molly Reilly received her initial flying instruction with the Royal Canadian Air Force.**

Before she demobilized in 1946, she also earned her commercial licence. In 1948 Molly gained instructor's rating and was hired as an instructor and charter pilot. She upgraded her qualifications, completing an advanced instrument flying course, a float plane course, and qualifying for a British commercial pilot's licence.

As chief flying instructor for Canadian Aircraft Renters in 1954, Molly was the first Canadian woman to gain Class 1 instrument rating and an airline transport licence. She made captain, flying heavy twin-engined aircraft and participating in the company's air ambulance service. In 1959 she married Jack Reilly, co-piloting with him in the Arctic, and then became chief pilot for Canadian Utilities. In 1973 Molly was named a member of Canada's Aviation Hall of Fame: "Her dedication to flight, her self-set demands for perfection, the outstanding abilities she has developed despite adversity, have made her a guiding light in aviation circles."

# Frances Williams Fraser 1923-1989

**Growing up on the Blackfoot reserve and learning to speak Blackfoot, Frances Williams became interested in stories the elders told. When they feared their knowledge would be lost, the elders asked her to write their stories down, and Frances began her life's vocation, recording Blackfoot legends and songs.**

Frances' father was assistant agent to the Blackfoot and her mother was a correspondent for the *Calgary Herald*. Their farm was on the edge of the Blackfoot Reserve at Cluny. After Frances married Frank Fraser and moved southeast of High River, she continued writing about Blackfoot legends for the *Globe and Mail* and other papers and magazines. Over the years she became an authority on Blackfoot legends and language, writing two books, *The Bear That Stole the Chinook,* and *The Wind Along the River*, and compiling a 270-page dictionary of the old form of Blackfoot.

She preserved hundreds of legends and songs in writing and on tape, striving to tell the Blackfoot stories the way the original storytellers did, with particular care for accuracy and exact meanings in her translations. Frances was interested in other aspects of the Blackfoot culture and did beautiful beadwork.

# Myrtle Sayers Leadlay (born 1923)

**Myrtle Leadlay's chief contribution has been her continuous effort to develop public appreciation for the ability and desire of handicapped people to share in community life as ordinary citizens.**

Myrtle began a long career in community recreation in 1960 when she became playground and play school supervisor for Jasper Place. She graduated from a provincial government director's course in 1964. Jasper Place amalgamated with Edmonton that year, and Myrtle became a city employee. As director of day camps, hobbies, and nature programs, she became aware of the need for recreational activities for disabled people. She initiated several, including a day camp, a teen club, and an adults club.

In 1969 Edmonton appointed Myrtle director of its program for the handicapped, becoming the first municipal body in western Canada to create such a recreation program. There were, in fact, few such programs of any significance in the country. Under Myrtle's leadership, the city program for special groups was so successful it has been used as a guide and pattern across Canada. Myrtle initiated a pre-school for disabled children, an amputee ski club, day camps, and a riding club. She developed the Alberta Special Games.

# Hope Large Johnson

**Hope Large Johnson turned a casual interest in Alberta fossils into a lifetime of work. When someone mentioned fossils to her in 1948, Hope began watching out for them. Finding large quantities of marine fossils in the gravel pits near her home, she sent a box of samples to the geology department at the University of Alberta (U of A), and received encouragement.**

Fossils soon became more than a hobby to her. Hope collected specimens throughout southern Alberta and worked with field parties from the university and museums across Canada. Many Canadian and United States paleontologists recognized this self-taught enthusiast as a colleague and a professional, and Hope worked for the Medicine Hat Museum and for four summers as curator at Dinosaur Provincial Park.

Hope was well known as a nature artist, and her paintings and drawings were widely exhibited. She drew a variety of fossil vertebrates from her own collection and the collections of Canadian museums. In the 1970s she collaborated with Dr. J.E. Storer, Provincial Museum, Edmonton, turning a series of drawings into an identification manual of Alberta's vertebrate fossils, *A Guide to Alberta's Vertebrate Fossils from the Age of Dinosaurs.*

# Anne Jaksa Lazlock (born 1924)

By 1956, Canada had long been home to Anne Jaksa Lazlock, but she never forgot what it was like to be a newcomer in a foreign land. That's why she met every train and plane bringing refugees from the Hungarian Revolution to Edmonton. She helped find homes and jobs for them, explained Canadian ways, and reassured them in their own language. It was just one more example of Anne's work on behalf of Hungarian communities and culture in Canada.

She came with her Hungarian parents to Calgary when she was four, attended school and business college there, and married a fellow Hungarian. When they moved to Edmonton, Anne continued her work at all levels of the Catholic Women's League, but she added more and more projects concerning the preservation of ethnic cultures. She organized an annual Hungarian fashion show, folk dancing groups, a cookbook entitled *Hungarian Rhapsody*, craft shows, and finally a television show that featured new Canadians from many countries. No wonder she was on the executive of the Canadian Citizenship Council in Edmonton and Calgary for 20 years.

In 1976, Anne received an Alberta Achievement Award.

# Marlene Kerkovius Mantel

Marlene Kerkovius Mantel knew what it was like to be a newcomer in a strange land. At the beginning of World War II, she and her German-Baltic parents were forced to move to Germany from Latvia.

After the war, Marlene married Rolf Mantel in Germany, and they moved to Edmonton – their own choice this time, but it was an adjustment nevertheless. Marlene's brother, who was a founder of the Canadian Baltic Immigrant Aid Society, made the adjustment easier when he asked his sister to "do something" for German speaking senior citizens in Edmonton. Starting with an initial list of some 250 people, Marlene ended up with more than 400 seniors for whom she arranged coffee parties, special events, speakers, whatever she could figure out.

Help for these events came from her "all-round helpers," a youth group who turned up at her events and worked in the kitchen, cleaned up, or helped entertain. In turn, Marlene helped them organize their activities and served as chaperone when needed. The German Canadian Association of Alberta recognized Marlene's work with young and old alike when they presented her with a scroll in 1975 for outstanding services to the community.

# Sheila MacKay Russell

**First a nurse, then a best selling author – that was Sheila MacKay Russell's career path.** She took nurses training at Calgary General Hospital, then obtained her diploma in public health nursing from the University of Alberta. Thus armed, Sheila went out into the work world as first a hospital nurse, then a public health nurse in rural areas, and finally an administrator in the provincial Department of Health.

When she married George Russell in 1947 and resigned from the formal work world, she took all her nursing experience and turned it into *A Lamp Is Heavy*, a book about the trials and tribulations of a student nurse. It was so popular that it was translated into seven languages, serialized in magazines, sold through book clubs, and finally made into a movie by the J. Arthur Rank film company in 1956. The movie retained the name A Lamp is Heavy.

Sheila's second book, *Living Earth*, also sold well, but nothing could eclipse the popularity of her first. After the books came a short story series for *Chatelaine* magazine, radio scripts, newspaper articles, and editing assignments. Sheila's writing has been reprinted in England, Australia, and South Africa.

# Anne Bulva Boras

**Yugoslavian-born Anne Boras helped turn her family's Picture Butte farm into a showcase for mixed farming and found time for community involvement.**

Anne came to Canada with her family. In 1950, she married Walter Boras, who was also Yugoslavian-born. The couple raised five children. Walter had a quarter section of land when they married, and over the years, the couple expanded the farm. They successfully integrated irrigation sugar-beet production with a range cow-calf and feedlot operation. In 1967, they were awarded a Master Farm designation. To win the award, a family had to have been on the same land, successfully, for 20 years and to have demonstrated citizenship and community leadership.

The Boras family continued to develop the farm after 1967, introducing European cattle to the cattle operation, installing natural gas, and substituting a sprinkler system for the old irrigation system. Besides caring for her family and a large garden, Anne was active in the Catholic Women's League and the Home and School Association. She encouraged her children's community involvement and sang in her church choir. Both Anne and Walter were active in the Coyote Flats Historical Society.

# Joyce Doolittle  (born 1928)

**Writer, actress, director, and producer, Joyce Doolittle believes in children's theatre, Canadian plays, and avante guarde productions. She has been involved with the founding and promotion of many Calgary theatre developments.**

Before coming to Calgary in 1960, Joyce was already deeply involved in theatre. She attended Ithaca College in New York state, where she was attracted to children's theatre. There she met her husband, Quentin. They both studied on scholarship at Indiana University, where Joyce wrote a master's thesis on creative drama for children.

In Calgary, her theatre involvement expanded even further. Joyce founded the Calgary Youth Drama Society. She initiated the development of the Pumphouse Theatre – a performing arts center for young people. She organized the creative dramatics program at the University of Calgary. She founded the Canadian branch of the World Organization for Theatre for Young Audiences. She was a member of the board of the Mac 14 Society, an amateur community theatre which turned professional and evolved into Theatre Calgary. She was one of the original board members when Alberta Theatre Projects was founded.

# Lori Borgens Johnson, C.M.  (died in 1996)

**Lori Borgens Johnson recognized the possibility of art helping to overcome racial and social tensions in the Cold Lake area, and did something about it.**

Lori studied art in Europe while her husband Jim was posted overseas with the Canadian Armed Services. When they were posted to Cold Lake, she started teaching art to adults. When she was approached by a Metis youngster about joining the class, Lori saw art in a new light. Recognizing the need for programs that might defuse social and racial tensions, she organized International Developmental Education through Art (IDEA). Its primary goal was to provide native youth with assistance and guidance through creative arts and crafts.

By 1972, IDEA had formal approval, and a year later 300 students and 16 instructors were at work. A campaign raised funds for a new building, the Catharine Whyte Multicultural Center. IDEA has been integrated into the local curriculum. Lori was awarded an Order of Canada in 1975 for the success of her work in integrating native, Metis, and white children in the Cold Lake area. Lori and Jim are the parents of two daughters.

# Caen Gladstone Bly (born 1944)

**Caen Bly served as editor of the *Kainai News* on the Blood Reserve for 12 years. Under her direction and despite funding and publishing problems, the newspaper grew to be the largest native newspaper in Canada, its scope reaching far beyond reserve affairs to national and international matters.**

Granddaughter of Senator James Gladstone, Jennifer Caen Gladstone was educated in Cardston and Calgary. She studied social welfare at Mount Royal College. In 1963 she married Ted Bly, manager of her father's cow-calf operation. For the next five years she assisted him, riding the range, branding, calving, and cooking for the ranch hands. In 1967, when a newspaper was proposed to improve reserve communication, she was asked to edit it.

Caen finds great satisfaction in sports, including rodeo, softball, basketball, swimming, skiing and golf. "I have found that through sports one really learns to live. You learn to know defeat, victory, sportsmanship, and brotherhood . . . how to compete. You have to choose whether you want to be a winner or a loser. A winner is not one who always wins in the field of life, but one who gains satisfaction in doing his personal best."

# Marilyn Lebsack Onofrychuk (born 1944)

**Marilyn Lebsack Onofrychuk not only won the world wheat championship at the 1973 Royal Winter Fair in Toronto, the first woman to do so, but she also went back and took the title again two years later.**

Alberta born, Marilyn grew up in the Vulcan area. She followed in her father, Harold Hansen's footsteps as he was both world flax and world wheat champion several times over. Marilyn began showing wheat in junior classes at Calgary and Lethbridge fairs early on. She was married to Richard Lebsack and they were farming 2,000 acres near Vulcan when her sample of Chinook hard red spring wheat won the 1973 championship. Marilyn explained she worked with the winning grain four or five hours a day, five days a week for three weeks before she finally decided on her 10-pound sample.

Marilyn won and was named Wheat Queen again in 1975. She was interested in more than wheat, however. She held offices with the United Church Women, the Vulcan Lionettes, and the Eastern Star lodge. She taught young people at the United Church, and she also taught swimming.

**A**
Andrews Catherine Brodie 54
Archer, Violet 86
Armstrong, Ellen Lowe 81
Atkinson Susan Wright 63
Attrux, Laura Margaret 79

**B**
Bagnall, Lucy Lowe 36
Baldwin, Nora Gladstone 94
Barclay Catherine 95
Barclay Mary 95
Barrett Elizabeth 8
Barss Violet McCully 40
Belyea Helen Reynolds 85
Bielish Martha Palamaraek 88
Biron, Antoinette Babin 60
Birtles Mary Ellen 11
Bly Caen Gladstone 101
Boras Anne Bulva 99
Borgal Pearl Edmanson 82
Bowman Maude Cowling 25
Bowker Mary Marjorie 91
Brainard Dora Brock 29
Bray Jemima McKay 9
Brick Sarah Lendrum 26
Broder Annie Glenn 17
Brown Annora 63

**C**
Calder Grace Louise Reynolds 14
Campbell Anne 84
Card Zina Young 5
Carmichael Beatrice VanLoon 66
Carse Ruth 91
Carson Marion Coutts 15
Casselman Cora Watt 44
Chapman Jessie Marie 33
Charette Marie Louise Desrosiers 45
Chittick Rae McIntyre 64
Church Jessie Louise Purves 50
Chrzanowski Maria Agopsowicz 86
Cody Mary Barter 51
Cohen Martha Block 92
Condell Abigail Edith Blow 21

Conquest Mary Owen 24
Coupland Mary 65
Crowchild Violet Otter 92
Curtis Alice 27

**D**
Dickie Donald James 37
Dobbs Mildred 29
Doolittle Joyce 100
Donahue Alice Baird 75
Dover Mary Cross 72

**E**
Edwards Henrietta Muir 3
Edwards Martha Murphy 47
Egbert Gladys McKelvie 55

F
Fish Aileen Hackett 61
Fisher Olive Margaret 46
Fraser Frances Williams 96

G
Gaetz Annie Siddall 36
Gaetz Caroline Hamilton 4
Gale Annie 28
Gibson Helen Beny 70
Gorman Ruth Peacock 89
Gowan Elsie Park 73
Gravel Marie-Anne LeBlanc 33
Greenham Margaret Haskins 31
Gunn Catherine Nichols 44

**H**
Haakstad Johanna 39
Hall Gertrude 70
Hansen Wilma Swinarton 73
Hoare Jean Patterson 87
Harder Sara Lehn 84
Hardisty Eliza McDougall 3
Hargreave Alexandra Sissons 7
Haynes Elizabeth Sterling 61
Hill Agnes Ashton 52
Hills Signe Spokeli 42
Holmes Maud Lewis 59